The Knight of Malta

John Fletcher

ISBN: 978-1-84902-170-8

The Knight of Malta

THE KNIGHT OF MALTA:

A TRAGI-COMEDY.

The Commendatory Verses by Gardiner ascribe this play (which was first printed in the folio of 1647) to Fletcher alone. It hath not been acted within the memory of any person now living, nor do we know of any alteration of it.

PERSONS REPRESENTED.

VALETTA, *the Grand-master of Malta.*
MIRANDA, *an Italian Gentleman, the* Knight of Malta.
ASTORIUS,} *two Knights of the Order.*
CASTRIOT,}
MOUNTFERRAT, *a Knight of the Order, but a Villain.*
GOMERA, *a deserving Spanish Gentleman.*
NORANDINE, *a valiant merry Dane, Commander-in-chief of the Gallies of Malta.*
COLONNA, *alias* ANGELO, *a Captive redeemed from the Gallies, and beloved of Miranda.*
ROCCA, *Servant and Instrument to Mount-* [ferrat.
Two Bishops.
Soldiers.

Corporal.
Prisoners.
Two Marshals.
Doctor.
One of the Esguard.
Servants.

ORIANA, *Sister to Valetta, and Wife of Gomera.*
VELLEDA, *Attendant on Oriana.*
ZANTHIA, *alias* ABDELLA, *a Moor, Servant to Oriana.*
LUCINDA, *a beautiful Turkish Woman, contracted to Angelo, Prisoner to Miranda.*
Two Gentlewomen.

SCENE, *Malta.*

ACT I.

SCENE I.

Enter Mountferrat.

Mountferrat. **D**ARES she despise me thus? me, that with spoil
And hazardous exploits, full sixteen years
Have led (as hand-maids) Fortune, Victory,
Whom the Maltezi call my servitors?
Tempests I have subdued, and fought them calm,
Out-lighten'd light'ning in my chivalry,
Rid (tame as Patience) billows that kick'd Heav'n,
Whistled enraged Boreas 'till his gusts
Were grown so gentle, that he seem'd to sigh,
Because he could not shew the air my keel;
And yet I cannot conquer her bright eyes,
Which, tho' they blaze, both comfort and invite; [ear,
Neither by force, nor fraud, pass thro' her
Whose guard is only blushing Innocence,
To take the least possession of her heart.
Did I attempt her with a thread-bare name,
Un-napt with meritorious actions,
She might with colour disallow my suit:
But, by the honour of this Christian cross,
(In blood of infidels so often dyed,
Which mine own soul and sword hath fixed here,
And neither favour, nor birth's privilege)
Oriana shall confess, (altho' she be
Valetta's sister, our Grand-master here)
The wages of scorn'd love is baneful hate,
And, if I rule not her, I'll rule her fate.

Enter Rocca.

Rocca, my trusty servant, welcome!
Rocca. Sir,
I wish my news deserv'd it! Hapless I,
That, being lov'd and trusted, fail to bring
The loving answer that you do expect.
Mountf. Why speak'st thou from me? thy pleas'd eyes send forth
Beams brighter than the star that ushers day;
Thy smiles restore sick expectation. [mine.
Rocca. I bring you, sir, her smiles, not

Mountf. Her smiles?
Why, they are presents for kings' eldest sons:
Great Solyman, that wearies his hot eyes
But to peruse his deck'd seraglio,
When from the number of that night, in his pride
He chuseth one for that night, in his pride
Of them, wives, wealth, is not so rich as I
In this one smile, from Oriana sent.

Rocca. Sir, fare you well!

Mountf. Oh, Rocca! thou art wise,
And wouldst not have the torrent of my joy
Ruin me headlong! Aptly thou conceiv'st,
If one reviving smile can raise me thus,
What trances will the sweet words which
　　thou bring'st
Cast me into. I felt, my dearest friend,
(No more my servant) when I employ'd thee,
That knew'st to look and speak as lovers
　　should,
And carry faithfully thy master's sighs,
That it must work some heat in her cold heart;
And all my labours now come fraughted home
With ten-fold prize.

Rocca. Will you yet hear me?

Mountf. Yes:
But take heed, gentle Rocca, that thou dost
Tenderly by degrees assault mine ears
With her consent, now to embrace my love;
For thou well know'st I've been so plung'd,
　　so torn
With her resolved reject, and neglect,
That to report her soft acceptance now
Will stupify sense in me, if not kill.
Why shew'st thou this distemper?

Rocca. Draw your sword, [you,
And, when I with my breath have blasted
Kill me with it:
I bring you smiles of pity, not affection,
For such she sent.

Mountf. Oh! can she pity me?
Of all the paths lead to a woman's love,
Pity's the straightest.

Rocca. Waken, sir, and know
That her contempt (if you can name it so)
Continues still; she bids you throw your pearl
Into strong streams, and hope to turn them so,
Ere her to foul dishonour; write your plaints
In rocks of coral grown above the sea;
Them hope to soften to compassion,
Or change their modest blush to love-sick
　　pale,
Ere work her to your impious requests.
All your loose thoughts she chides you home
　　again,
But with such calm behaviour, and mild looks,
She gentlier denies than others grant,
For just as others love, so doth she hate.
She says, that by your order you are bound
From marrying ever, and much marvels then
You would thus violate her, and your own
　　faith,
That being the virgin you should now protect.
Hitherto, she professes, sh' has conceal'd
Your lustful batt'ries; but the next, she vows,
(In open hall, before the honour'd cross,

And her great brother) she will quite forsake,
Calling for justice, to your utter shame.

Mountf. Hence! find the Blackamoor that
　　waits upon her,
Bring her unto me; she doth love me yet,
And I must her now, at least seem to do.
Cupid, thy brands that glow thus in my veins,
I will with blood extinguish!—Art not gone!
　　　　　　　　　　　　　　[*Exit Rocca.*
Shall my desires, like beggars, wait at door,
Whilst any others revel in her breast?
Sweat on, my spirits! Know, thou trick'd-up
　　toy,
My love's a violent flood, where thou art falln,
Playing with which tide th' hadst been gently
　　toss'd,
But, crossing it, thou art o'erwhelm'd and lost.

Enter Astorius and Castriot.

Cast. Monsieur, good day!

Asto. Good morrow, valiant knight!
What, are you for this great solemnity
This morn intended?

Mountf. What solemnity?

Asto. Th' investing of the martial Spaniard,
Peter Gomera, with our Christian badge.

Cast. And young Miranda, the Italian;
Both which, with wondrous prowess and great
　　luck,
Have dar'd and done for Malta such high
　　feats,
That not one fort in it but rings their name
As loud as any man's.

Mountf. As any man's?
Why, we have fought for Malta.

Asto. Yes, Mountferrat,
No bold knight ever past you; but we wear
The dignity of Christians on our breasts,
And have a long time triumph'd for our con-
　　quests: [yet
These conquer'd a long time, not triumph'd

Mountf. Astorius, you're a most indul-
　　gent knight,
Detracting from yourself, to add to others.
You know this title is the period
To all our labours, the extremity
Of that tall pyramid, where honour hangs;
Which we with sweat and agony have reach'd,
And should not then so easily impart
So bright a wreath to every cheap desert.

Cast. How is this Frenchman chang'd,
　　Astorius!
Some sullen discontent possesses him,
That makes him envy what he heretofore
Did most ingenuously but emulate.

Mount. Oh, furious desire, how like a
　　whirlwind
Thou hurriest me beyond mine honour's point!
Out of my heart, base lust! or, heart, I vow
Those flames that heat me thus, I'll burn
　　thee in. [*Aside.*

Asto. Do you observe him?

Mountf. What news of the Dane?
That valiant captain Norandine?

Cast. He fights still,

In view o'th' town; he plays the devil with
And they, the Turks with him.   ['em,
    Mountf. They're well met then;
'Twere sin to sever 'em. Pish—woman—
    memory—
'Would one of ye would leave me!   [*Aside.*
    Asto. Six fresh gallies.
I in St. Angelo from the promontory
This morn descried, making a girdle for him;
But our Great-master doth intend relief
This present meeting. Will you walk along?
    Mountf. Hum—I have read, ladies enjoy'd
    have been   [names,
The gulphs of worthiest men, buried their
Their former valour, bounty, beauty, virtue,
And sent them stinking to untimely graves.
I that cannot enjoy, by her disdain,
Am like to prove as wretched. Woman then
Checking, or granting, is the grave of men.
    [*Aside.*
    Asto. He's saying of his prayers sure.
    Cust. Will you go, sir?   [ported
    Mountf. I cry you mercy! I am so trans-
(Your pardon, noble brothers) with a business
That doth concern all Malta, that I am
(Anon you'll hear it) almost blind and deaf—
(Lust neither sees nor hears aught but itself)—
But I will follow instantly. Your cross.
    Asto. Not mine.   [*Cross dropt.*
    Cust. Nor mine; 'tis yours.
    Asto. Cust. Good morrow, brother. [*Exe.*
    Mountf. White innocent sign, thou dost
    abhor to dwell   [breast,
So near the dim thoughts of this troubled
And grace these graceless projects of my
    heart!

        Enter Zanthia, alias Abdella.

Yet I must wear thee, to protect my crimes,
If not for conscience, for hypocrisy;
Some churchmen so wear cassocks. Oh, my
    Zanthia,
My pearl, that scorns a stain! I much repent
All my neglects; let me, Ixion like,
Embrace my black cloud. since my Juno is
So wrathful, and averse: Thou art more soft
And full of dalliance than the fairest flesh,
And far more loving.
    Zant. Ay, you say so now;
But, like a property, when I have serv'd
Your turns, you'll cast me off, or hang me up
For a sign somewhere.
    Mountf. May my life then forsake me,
Or, from my expected bliss, be cast to hell!
    Zant. My tongue, sir, cannot lisp to meet
    you so,
Nor my black cheek put on a feigned blush,
To make me seem more modest than I am.
This ground-work will not bear adult'rate red,
Nor artificial white, to cozen love.   [teeth,
These dark locks are not purchas'd, nor these
For ev'ry night they are my bedfellows;
No bath, no blanching water, smoothing oils,

Doth mend me up; and yet, Mountferrat,
    know,
I am as full of pleasure in the touch
As e'er a white-fac'd puppet of 'em all,
Juicy, and firm; unfledge them of their tires,
Their wires, their partlets, pins, and perriwigs,
And they appear like bald-cootes, in the nest:
I can as blithly work in my love's bed,
And deck thy fair neck with these jetty chains,
Sing thee asleep, being wearied; and, refresh'd,
With the same organ, steal sleep off again.
    Mountf. Oh, my black swan, sleeker than
    cygnet's plush[1],
Sweeter than is the sweet of pomander,
Breath'd like curl'd Zephyrus, cooling limon-
    trees,   [grove!
Straight as young pines, or cedars in the
Quickly descend, lovers' best canopy,
Still Night, for Zanthia doth enamour me
Beyond all continence! Perpetrate, dear
    wench,
What thou hast promis'd, and I vow by Heav'n,
Malta, I'll leave in it my honours here,
And in some other country, Zanthia make
My wife, and my best fortune.
    Zant. From this hope,
Here is an answer to that letter, which
I lately shew'd you, sent from Tripoly,
By the great basha, which importunes her
Love unto him, and treachery to the island;
Which will she undertake, by Mahomet
The Turk there vows, on his blest Alcoran,
Marriage unto her: This the Master knows,
But is resolv'd of her integrity,
As well he may, sweet lady; yet, for love,
For love of thee, Mountferrat, (oh! what
    chains
Of deity, or duty can hold love?)
I have this answer fram'd, so like her hand
As if it had been moulded off, returning
The basha's letter safe into her pocket.
What you will do with it, yourself best knows.
Farewell! keep my true heart, keep true your
    vows.   [*Exit.*
    Mountf. 'Till I be dust, my Zanthia, be
    confirm'd.   [lips.—
Sparrows, and doves, sit coupling 'twixt thy
It is not love, but strong libidinous will
That triumphs o'er me; and to satiate that,
What diff'rence 'twixt this Moor, and her fair
    dame?
Night makes their hues alike, their use is so;
Whose hand's so subtle he can colours name,
If he do wink, and touch 'em? Lust being
    blind,
Never in women did distinction find. [*Exit.*

SCENE II.

Enter two Gentlewomen.

    1 *Gent.* But i'faith dost thou think my lady
Was never in love?
    2 *Gent.* I rather think she was ever

---

[1] Silkner *than cygnet's plush.*] So first folio.   *Sympson.*

In love; in perfect charity[1], I mean,
With all the world.

1 Gent. A most Christian answer,
I promise you. But I mean in love
With a man. [have her

2 Gent. With a man? what else? wouldst
In love with a beast?

1 Gent. You are somewhat quick;
But if she were, it were no precedent:
Did you never read of Europa
The fair, that leapt a bull, that leapt the sea,
That swam to land, and then leapt her?

2 Gent. Oh, heavens! a bull?

1 Gent. Yes, a white bull.

2 Gent. Lord! how could she sit him?
Where did she hold? [time,

1 Gent. Why, by the horn; since which
No woman, almost, is contented 'till
She have a horn of her own to hold by.

2 Gent. Thou
Art very knavish.

1 Gent. And thou very foolish.
But, sirrah, why dost thou not marry?

2 Gent. Because
I would be no man's looking-glass.

1 Gent. As how?

2 Gent. As thus; there is no wife (if she
Be good and true, will honour and obey)
But must reflect the true countenance of
Her husband upon him: If he look sad upon
    her,
She must not look merrily upon him; if he
Look merrily, she must not sorrowfully;
Else she is a false glass, and fit for
Nothing but breaking: His anger must be
Her discontent, his pleasure her delight:
If he weep, she must cry;
If he laugh, she must shew her teeth;
If he be sick, she must not be in health;
If he eat caudles, she must eat pottage; she
Must have no proper passion of her own!
And is not this a tyranny?

1 Gent. Yes, i'faith! [then
Marriage may well be call'd a yoke! Wives
Are but like superficial lines in geometry,
That have no proper motion of their own,

But as their bodies (their husbands) move. Yet
I know some wives, that are never freely
    merry,
Nor truly pleas'd, but when they're furthest
Their husbands. [off

2 Gent. That's because the moon
Governs 'em; which hath most light and shines
Brightest, the more remote it is from the sun;
And, contrary, is more sullen, dim, and shews
Least splendor, when it is nearest.

1 Gent. But if I were to marry,
I would marry a fair effeminate fool.

2 Gent. Why?

1 Gent. Because I would lead the blind
    whither I list. [for money,

2 Gent. And I the wisest man I could get
Because I had rather follow the clear-sighted
Bless me from a husband that sails by his

1 Gent. Why? [wife's compass!

2 Gent. Why, 'tis ten to one but she
Breaks his head in her youth; and, when she
    is old, [too!
She'll never leave 'till she has broke his back

1 Gent. But what scurvy knights have we
    here in Malta[2], [allegiance
That when they are dub'd take their oath of
To live poor, and chastly, ever after?

2 Gent. 'Faith,
Many knights in other nations (I have heard)
Are as poor as ours; marry, where one of 'em
Has taken the oath of chastity, we want
A new Columbus to find out.

Enter Zanthia.

Zant. Hist, wenches!
My lady calls; she's entering the terrace,
To see the show.

1 Gent. Oh, black pudding!

2 Gent. My little labour in vain! [*Exeunt.*

SCENE III.

*Enter above, Oriana, Zanthia, and two Gen-
tlewomen; beneath, Valetta, Mountferrat,
Astorius, Castriot, Gomera, Miranda, At-
tendants of Knights, &c.*

Mountf. Are you there, lady?

---

[1] *2 Gent. I rather think she was ever in love, in perfect charity.*
1 Gent. I mean, with all the world.
2 Gent. A most Christian answer, I promise you; but, &c.
2 Gent. With a man] Corrected in 1750.

[2] *Broke his back to——*
But what scurvy *knight* have *you* here in Malta, &c.
Enter Zanthia.
*Zan. Hist, wenches: my lady calls, she's ent'ring
The terrass, to see the show.*
1 Gent. Oh black pudding.
2 Gent. My little labour in vain.
1 Gent. But what scurvy knights have we here in Malta, that, &c.] This confusion and
repetition appear in all the editions but the present. We apprehend there can be no doubt
but Zanthia's entry, and the five following lines, should be removed to the conclusion of the
scene, which hitherto ended with the words, *Columbus to find out.* The &c. (with the sense-
less variation of the words) induces us to think, that the first occurrence of the reiterated
line was meant as a direction for the performer to pass on to that passage beginning, *But
what scurvy, &c.*

Ori. Thou'rt a naughty man;
Heav'n mend thee!

Val. Our great meeting, princely brothers,
Ye holy soldiers of the Christian-Cross,
Is to relieve our captain Norandine;
Now fighting for Valetta with the Turk[4];
A valiant gentleman, a noble Dane
As e'er the country bred, endanger'd now
By fresh supply of head-bound infidels[5].
Much means, much blood this warlike Dane
hath spent
T' advance our flag above their horned moons,
And oft hath brought in profitable conquest:
We must not see him perish in our view.
How far off fight they?

Mir. Sir, within a league.   [venting

Val. 'Tis well. Our next occasion of con-
Are these two gentlemen, standing in your
(Ye noble props of Malta!) royally   [sight;
Descended are they both, valiant as War[6],
Miranda, and Gomera: Full ten years
They've serv'd this island, perfected exploits
Matchless, and infinite; they're honest, wise,
Not empty of one ornament of man.
Most eminent agents were they in that
slaughter,
That great marvellous slaughter of the Turks,
Before St. Elme, where five and twenty thou-
sand
Fell, for five thousand of our Christians.
These ripe considerations moving us,
Having had your allowance on their worths[6],
Here we would call 'em to our brotherhood!
If any therefore can their manners tax,
Their faith, their chastity, any part of life,
Let 'em speak now.

Asto. None does.

All. None can, Great-master.

Val. The dignity then dignify, by them[7],
As their reward. Tender Miranda first
(Because he is to succour Norandine)
Our sacred robe of knighthood, our white cross
(The holy cognizance of him we serve),
The sword, the spurs.

Mir. Grave, and most honour'd Master,
With humble duty, and my soul's best thanks
To you, and all this famous conventicle,
Let me with modesty refuse acceptance

Of this high order! I, alas, am yet
Unworthy, and uncapable of such honour;
That merit, which with favour you enlarge,
Is far, far short, of this propos'd reward.
Who takes upon him such a charge as this,
Must come with pure thoughts, and a gather'd
That time nor all occasions ever may [mind,
After disperse, or stain. Did this title here
Of knighthood, ask no other ornaments
Than other countries, glitt'ring show, poor
pride,
A jingling spur, a feather, a white hand,
A frizzled hair, powder[8], perfumes, and lust,
Drinking sweet wines, surfeits, and ignorance,
Rashly and eas'ly should I venture on't;
But this requires another kind of man.

Mountf. A staid and mature judgment!
speak on, sir.

Mir. May't please you then t' allow me
some small time
To rectify myself for that high seat,
Or give my reasons to the contrary.
I' th' mean space, to dismiss me to the aid
Of Norandine: My ships ride in the bay
Ready to disembogue, tackled, and mann'd
Even to my wishes.

Mountf. His request
Is fair and honest.

Val. At your pleasure go.   [you,

Mir. I humbly take my leave of all: Of
My noble friend Mountferrat! Gracious
mistress—   [dier!
Oh, that auspicious smile doth arm your sol-
Who fights for those eyes, and this sacred
cross,
Can neither meet sad accident, nor loss!
[*Exit.*

Ori. The mighty master of that livery,
Conduct thee safely to these eyes again!

Mountf. Blows the wind that way?

Val. Equally belov'd,
Equally meriting, Gomera, you
Without excuse receive that dignity,   [you.
Which our provincial chapter hath decreed

Gom. Great-master of Jerus'lem's Hospital,
From whence to Rhodes this blest fraternity
Was driven, but now among the Maltese
stands,

[4] *Now fighting* for *Valetta.*] Sympson asks, 'But was Norandine then fighting only for
'the Grand-master?' Answering himself in the negative, he supposes a corruption, and reads,
'fighting 'fore Valetta.' We see no need for variation, the sense being, that he is fighting
for Valetta, upon the safety of which town their own security depends,

[5] *Head-bound.*] i. e. turban'd, as in Othello.   *Theobald.*

[6] *Valiant* as War.] Sympson thinks this corrupt, and says, 'We must turn the *W* upside
down, and add an s.' and so substitute *Mars* for *Wars*; or else read, *Valiant* is *war*; 'or, if
such a liberty may be allowed, *a valiant pair.*' There needs no variation, since by *War* is
understood the *genius* or *god of war.*

[6] *Their worthies.*] First folio. Probably wrote, '*these* worthies.'

[7] *The dignity then* dignifie, *by them*
    Is *their reward.*] So first folio. Sympson proposes reading,
        '———— then *dignified* by them,
        ' Is *their reward.*'

[8] *A frizzled hair,* powder'd, *perfumes,* &c.] Mr. Seward reads with me thus,
        ' A frizled hair, powder, perfumes,' &c.   *Sympson.*

Long may it flourish, whilst Gomera serves it,
But dares not enter further!
All. This is strange!
Val. What do you object?
Gom. Nothing against it, but myself, fair
I may not wear this robe. [knights;
Val. Express your reasons:
Doth any hid sin gnar your conscience?
Asto. Are you unstedfast in religion?
Cast. Or do you intend to forsake Malta
now,
And visit your own country, fruitful Spain?
Gom. Neither. good sir9.
Val. Then explicate your thoughts.
Gom. This then: I should be perjur'd to
receive it.
Once in Malta, your next city here,
When I was younger, read I the decrees
Touching this point, being ambitious then
T' approach it once. None but a gentleman
Can be admitted——
Val. That's no obstacle
In you.
Gom. I should be sorry that were it.—
No married man——
Mountf. You never felt that yoke.
Gom. None that hath been contracted——
Cast. Were you ever?
Gom. Nor married, nor contracted.—
None that ever
Hath vow'd his love to any womankind,
Or finds that secret fire within his thoughts:
Here I am cast; this article my heart
Objects against the title of my fame;
I am in love. Laugh not! tho' Time hath set
Some wrinkles in this face, and these curl'd
Will shortly dye into another hue, [locks
Yet, yet I am in love: (I'faith, you smile!)
What age, what sex, or what profession,
Divine or human, from the man that cries
For alms in the highway, to him that sings
At the high altar, and doth sacrifice,
Can truly say he knows not what is love?
Val. 'Tis honestly profess'd. With whom,
Gomera?
Name the lady, that with all advantage
We may advance your suit.
Gom. But will you, sir?
Val. Now by our holy rock, were it our
sister, [her.
Spaniard, I hold thee worthy; freely name
Gom. Be master of your word: It is she,
The matchless Oriana. [sir,
Val. Come down, lady.
You've made her blush: Let her consent, I
Make good my oath. [will
Mountf. Is't so?—Stay! I do love

So tenderly, Gomera, your bright fame10,
As not to suffer your perdition.
Gom. What means Mountferrat?
Mountf. This whole Auberge hath11——
(A guard upon this lady!) Wonder not!——

Enter Guard.

Ta'en publick notice of the basha's love
Of Tripoli unto her, and consented
She should return this answer, (as he writ
For her conversion, and betraying Malta)
She should advise him betray Tripoly,
And, turning Christian, he should marry her.
All. All this was so.
Mountf. How weakly does this court then
Send vessels forth to sea, to guard the land,
Taking such special care to save one bark,
Or strive to add fam'd men unto our cloak,
When they lurk in our bosoms would subvert
This state and us, presuming on their blood,
And partial indulgence to their sex?
Val. Who can this be?
Mountf. Your sister, great Valetta!
Which thus I prove: Demand the basha's
letter. [been mov'd
Ori. 'Tis here; nor from this pocket hath
Nor answer'd, nor perus'd, by——
Mountf. Do not swear;
Cast not away your fair soul; to your treason
Add not foul perjury!—Is this your hand?
Ori. 'Tis very like it.
Mountf. May it please the Master,
Confer these letters, and then read her answer,
Which I have intercepted. Pardon me,
Reverend Valetta, that am made the means
To punish this most beauteous treachery,
E'en in your sister, since in it I save
Malta from ruin: I am bolder in't,
Because it is so palpable, and withal
Know our Great-master to this country firm
As was the Roman Marcus, who spar'd not
As dear a sister in the publick cause.
Val. I am amaz'd! attend me.
[*Reads.*] ' Let your forces by the next even
' be ready; my brother feasts then; put in
' at St. Michaels; the ascent at that port is
' easiest; the keys of the castle you shall
' receive at my hands. That possess'd, you
' are lord of Malta, and may soon destroy all
' by fire; than which I am hotter, 'till I em-
' brace you. Farewell! Your wife, Oriana.'
From this time let me never read again.
Gentlew. 'Tis, certain, her hand.
Val. This letter too,
So close kept by herself, could not be answer'd
To every period thus, but by herself.
Ori. Sir, hear me!

9 *Never, good sir.*] The variation proposed by Seward.
10 *Your bright flame.*| Corrected in 1750.
11 *Auberge.*] In the *Anciens et Nouveaux Statuts de l'Ordre de Saint Jean de Jerusalem,*
the word *Auberge* frequently occurs; and, in the chapter *De la Signification des Termes,* is
thus explained: ' *Auberge* est un nom connu des François, des Espagnols, et des Italiens,
' pour signifier un lieu, ou l'on mange, et où l'on s'assemble Nation par Nation.' Vertot's
Histoire des Chevaliers de Malthe, tome vi. p. 266, edit. Paris, 1761.

Val. Peace! thou fair sweet bank of
   flowers,
Under whose beauty scorpions lie, and kill!
Wert thou akin to me in some new name
Dearer than sister, mother, or all blood,
I would not hear thee speak.—Bear her to
   prison!
So gross is this, it needs no formal course.
Prepare thyself; tomorrow thou shalt die.
  Ori. I die a martyr then, and a poor maid,
Almost i' faith as innocent as born!
Thou know'st thou'rt wicked, Frenchman;
  Heav'n forgive thee!   [*Exit.*
  All. This scene is strangely turned.
  Val. Yet can nature be
So dead in me!—I would my charge were off!
Mountferrat should perceive my sister had
A brother, would not live to see her die
Unfought for, since the statutes of our state
Allow, in case of accusations,
A champion to defend a lady's truth.—
Peter Gomera, thou hast lost thy wife:
Death pleads a precontract.
  Gom. I've lost my tongue,
My sense, my heart, and every faculty!
Mountferrat, go not up! With reverence
To our Great-master, and this consistory,
(I have consider'd it, it cannot be)
Thou art a villain and a forger,
A blood-sucker of innocence, an hypocrite,
A most unworthy wearer of our cross;
To make which good, take, if thou dar'st,
   that gage,
And, arm'd at all points like a gentleman,
Meet me tomorrow morning, where the Mas-
   ter
And this fraternity shall design [12]; where I
Will cram this slander back into thy throat,
And with my sword's point thrust it to thy
   heart,
The very nest where lust and slander breeds.
(Pardon my passion!) I will tear those spurs
Off from thy heels, and stick 'em in thy front,
As a mark'd villain!
  Mountf. This I look'd not for.—
Ten times more villain, I return my gage;
And crave the law of arms!
  Gom. 'Tis that I crave!
  All. It cannot be denied.
  Gom. Do not I know,
With thousand gifts and importunacies,
Thou often hast solicited this lady?
(Contrary to thy oath of chastity!)
Who ne'er disclosing this thy hot-rein'd lust [13],

Yet tender to prevent a publick scandal,
That Christendom might justly have impos'd
Upon this holy institution,
Thou now hast drawn this practice 'gainst her
To quit her charity.   [life,
  Mountf. Spaniard, thou liest!
  Asto. No more, Gomera! thou art granted
   combat.
And you, Mountferrat, must prepare against
Tomorrow morning, in the valley here,
Adjoining to St. George's Port. A lady,
In case of life, 'gainst whom one witness
May have her champion.   [comes,
  Val. And who hath most right,
With, or against our sister, speed in fight!
      [*Flourish. Exeunt.*

   Manet Mountferrat. Enter Rocca.
  Mountf. Rocca, the first news of Miran-
    s service
Let me have notice of.
  Rocca. You shall. The Moor
Waits you without.
  Mountf. Admit her.—Ha, ha, ha!
Oh, how my fancies run at tilt! Gomera
Loves Oriana; she, as I should guess,
Affects Miranda; these are two dear friends,
As firm, and full of fire, as steel and flint.
To make 'em so now, one against the other—

    Enter Zanthia.
Stay; let me like it better.—Zanthia,
First tell me this; did don Gomera use
To give his visits to your mistress?
  Zant. Yes,
And Miranda too, but severally.
  Mountf. Which did she most apply to?
  Zant. 'Faith, to neither:
Yet infinitely I've heard her praise them both,
And in that manner, that, were both one man,
I think she was in love with't.
  Mountf. Zanthia,
Another letter you must frame for me
Instantly, in your lady's character,
To such a purpose as I'll tell thee straight.
Go in, and stay me! Go, my tinder-box!
Cross lines I'll cross. So, so! my after-game
I must play better: Woman, I will spread
My vengeance over Malta, for thy sake!
Spaniard, Italian, like my steel and stone,
I'll knock ye thus together, wear ye out
To light my dark deeds, whilst I seem precise,
And wink, to save the sparkles from mine
   eyes.   [*Exeunt.*

---

  [12] *And this fraternity shall* design.] This word has its original signification to *appoint or
decree,* in Latin, *designare,* from whence *designator,* an herald.   *Seward.*
  [13] *Thy* hot reign'd *lust.*] Seward proposes reading, ' Thy *not* reign'd lust.' The variation
is from Sympson's conjecture.

ACT II.

SCENE I.

A Sea-fight within, Alarm.

Enter Norandine, Miranda, Soldiers, and Gentlemen.

Mir. HOW is it, sir?
  Nor. 'Pray set me down! I cool,
And my wounds smart.
 Mir. I hope yet,
Tho' there be many, there's none dangerous.
 Nor. I know not, nor I care not much; I
  got 'em   [geons
Like a too-forward fool; but I hope the sur-
Will take an order I sha'n't leave 'em so.
I make the rogues more work than all the
 island,
And yet they give me th' hardest words for
 my money.
 Mir. I'm glad ye are so sprightly! Ye
 fought bravely,   [nobly;
(Go call the surgeons, soldiers:) wondrous
Upon my life, I have not seen such valour,
Maintain'd so long, and to so large a ruin,
The odds so strong against ye.
 Nor. I thank ye,   [cour!
And thank ye for your help, your timely suc-
By th' mass, it came i' th' nick, sir, and well
 handled,   [else;
Stoutly, and strongly handled; we had duck'd
My Turk had turk'd me else: But h' has well
 paid for't.   [me!
Why, what a sign for an almanack h' has made

Enter Astorius.

Asto. I'm glad to find you here, sir; of
 necessity   [captain,
I must have come aboard else. And, brave
We all joy much in your fair victory,
And all the island speaks your valour nobly.
Have you brought the Turk in that you took?
 Mir. He rides there.
 Nor. If he were out again, the devil should
 bring him:
H' has truly circumcis'd me.
 Asto. I've a business
Which much concerns you, presently con-
 cerns you;
But not this place nor people: 'Pray ye draw
 off, sir!
For 'tis of that weight to you——
 Mir. I'll wait on you.—
I must crave leave awhile; my care dwells
 with you,
And I must wait myself——
 Nor. Your servant, sir.
 Mir. Believe I shall, and what my love
 can minister—
Keep your stout heart still——
 Nor. That's my best physician!
       [*Exit Asto.*

Mir. And I shall keep your fame fair.
       [*Exit.*
 Nor. You're too noble.
A brave young fellow, of a matchless spirit!
He brought me off like thunder, charg'd and
 boarded,
As if he had been shot to save mine honour:
And when my fainting men, tir'd with their
 labour
And lack of blood, gave to the Turk assu-
 rance   [thus,
The day was his: when I was cut in shreds
And not a corn of powder left to bless us:
Then flew his sword in, then his cannon roar'd,
And let fly blood and death, in storms a-
 mongst 'em.   [too,
Then might I hear their sleepy prophet howl
And all their silver crescents then I saw
Like falling meteors spent, and set for ever
Under the cross of Malta: Death so wanton
I never look'd upon, so full of revel.—

Enter Surgeon.

I will not be dress'd yet.—Methought that
 fellow
Was fit for no conversation, nor no Christian,
That had not half his brains knock'd out, no
 soldier.
Oh, valiant young man, how I love thy virtue!
 1 Sold. 'Pray you, sir, be dress'd! alas, you
 bleed apace yet.
 Nor. 'Tis but the sweat of honour. Alas!
 thou milksop,
Thou man of marchpane, canst thou fear to
 see   [ger?
A few light hurts, that blush they are no big-
A few small scratches? Get ye a caudle, sirrah,
(Your finger aches) and let the old wives
 watch thee!
Bring in the booty, and the prisoners:
By Heav'n, I'll see 'em, and dispose 'em first,
Before I have a drop of blood wip'd from
 me! go.
 Surg. You'll faint, sir. [*Exeunt Soldiers.*
 Nor. No, you lie, sir, like an ass, sir!
I have no such pig's heart in my belly [14].
 Surg. By my life, captain,
These hurts are not to be jested with.
 Nor. If thou hadst 'em;
They're my companions, fool, my family:
I cannot eat nor sleep without their company.
Dost take me for St. Davy, that fell dead
With seeing of his nose bleed?

Enter Soldiers with booty.

 Surg. Here they come, sir:
But 'would you would be dress'd!
 Nor. Pox, dress thyself first!
Thou faint'st a great deal faster. What's all
 this?

---

[14] *I have no such pigs hurt in my belly.*] The correction is from Sympson's conjecture.

1 Sold. The money and the merchandize
ye took, sir.   [venture
Nor. A goodly purchase! Is't for this we
Our liberties and lives? What can all this do?
Get me some dozen surfeits, some seven
    fresh whores [15],
And twenty pot-allies, and then I'm virtuous.
Lay the knights' part by, and that to pay the
    soldier:
This is mine own; I think I have deserv'd it.—
Come; now look to me, and grope me like a
    chambermaid;
I'll neither start nor squeak.—What's that
    i' th' truss there?
2 Sold. 'Tis cloth of tissue, sir; and this
    is scarlet.
Nor. I shall look redder shortly then, I
    fear me,
And as a captain ought, a great deal prouder.
Can ye cure me of that crack, surgeon?
Surg. Yes, when your suit's at pawn, sir.
Nor. There's for your plaister.
A very learned surgeon!—What's in that pack
1 Sold. 'Tis English cloth.   [there?
Nor. That's a good wear indeed,
Both strong and rich; but it has a virtue,
A twang of the own country, that spoils all;
A man shall ne'er be sober in't. Where are
    the gentlemen   [fortunes?
That ventur'd with me, both their lives and
Come forward, my fair spirits! Norandine
Forgets his worth, when he forgets your va-
    lours.
You've lost an eye; I saw you face all hazards;
You've one left yet, to chuse your mistress.
You have your leg broke with a shot; yet,
    sitting,   [still.
I saw you make the place good with your pike
And your hand's gone; a good heart wants
    no instruments.   [arm;
Share that amongst ye: There's an eye; an
And that will bear you up, when your legs
    cannot.—   [low,
Oh, where's the honest sailor? that poor fel-
Indeed that bold brave fellow, that with his
    musquet   [off,
Taught them new ways how to put their caps
That stood the fire of all the fight, twice blown,
And twice I gave him drown'd?—Welcome
    ashore, knave!
Give me thy hand, if they be not both lost.
'Faith, thou art welcome! my tough knave,
    welcome!
Thou wilt not shrink i' th' washing.

Hold, there's a piece of scarlet; get thee hand-
And this to buy thee buttons.   [some;
Sailor. Thank you, captain.
Command my life at all hours.
Nor. Thou durst give it.—
You have deserv'd too?
3 Sold. We have seen the fight, sir. [eels,
Nor. Yes; coil'd up in a cable, like salt
Or buried low i' th' ballast: Do you call that
    fighting?
Where be your wounds? your knocks? your
    want of limbs, rogues?
Art not thou he that ask'd the master-gunner
Where thou might'st lie safest? and he strait
    answer'd,   [cannon,
Put thy head in that hole, new bor'd with a
For it was an hundred to one, another shot
    would not hit there?
Your wages you shall have; but for rewards
Take your own ways, and get ye to the ta-
    verns;
There, when ye're hot with wine, 'mongst
    your admirers,   [pleasures,
Take ships, and towns, and castles at your
And make the Great Turk shake at your
    valours.—Bring in
The prisoners. Now, my brave Mussulmans,

Enter Prisoners and Lucinda.

You that are lords o' th' sea, and scorn us
    Christians,   [here?
Which of your mangy lives is worth this hurt
Away to prison with 'em, see 'em safe!
You shall find we have gallies too, and slaves
    too.   [sir?
1 Sold. What shall be done with this woman,
Nor. Pox take her! [*Surgeons dress him.*
'Twas she that set me on to fight with these
    rogues!—   [now,
That ring-worm, rot it!—What can you do
With all your paintings, and your pouncings,
    lady,   [Cupid,
To restore my blood again? you, and your
That have made a carbonado of me—Plague
    take you,
You are too deep, you rogue!—This is thy
    work, woman,   [still!—
Thou lousy woman!—Death, you go too deep
The seeing of your simpering sweetness, you
    filly,   [jingling,
You tit, you tomboy! what can one night's
Or two, or ten, sweetheart, and 'oh, my dear
    chicken,'   [foremast,
Scratching my head, or fumbling with my

---

[15] *Get me —— some seven fresh whores,*
    And twenty pot-allies, and then I'm virtuous.] The oldest copy reads thus:
        'And twenty pot allies and *to*: and then,' &c.
Which would induce one to think the original might run so:
        'And twenty pot allies, And *two*.'
Two is often mistakenly wrote *too* in the oldest edition, and possibly might have been so
here.   *Sympson.*
    The meaning of the whole passage, we think, is this: 'What can all this money do? Get
'me surfeits, whores, and a score of pot-companions to cry me up!' *And to*, we think, is
corrupt, but not explained properly by Sympson.

Do me good now? You've powder'd me for
  one year: [beauty,
I am in souce, I thank you; thank your
Your most sweet beauty! Pox upon those
  goggles!
We cannot fight like honest men, for honour,
And quietly kill one another as we ought,
But in steps one of you; the devil's holiness
And you must have a dance. Away with her!
She stinks to me now.
  1 *Sold.* Shall I have her, captain?
  2 *Sold.* Or I?
  3 *Sold.* I'll marry her——
  4 *Sold.* Good captain, I——
  3 *Sold.* And make her a good Christian.
    Lay hands on her;
I know she's mine.
  2 *Sold.* I'll give my full share for her!
Have ye no manners, to thrust the woman so?
  Nor. Share her among ye;
And may she give ye as many hurts as I have,
And twice as many aches!
  Luc. Noble captain,   [wildness,
Be pleas'd to free me from these soldiers'
'Till I but speak two words.
  Nor. Now for your maidenhead!
You have your book; proceed.
  Luc. Victorious sir,
Seldom are seen in men so valiant,   [quer,
Minds so devoid of virtue; he that can con-
Should ever know how to preserve his con-
  quest;
'Tis but a base theft else: Valour's a virtue,
Crown of men's actions here; yours, as you
  make it.
And can you put so rough a foil as violence,
As wronging of weak woman, to your triumph?
  Nor. Let her alone!
  Luc. I've lost my husband, sir;   [not:
You feel not that: Him that I love; you care
When fortune falls on you thus, you may
  grieve too.
My liberty I kneel not for; mine honour
(If ever virtuous honour touch'd your heart
  yet)   [mother——
Make dear and precious, sir. You had a
  Nor. The roguy thing speaks finely, neat.
  Who took you?
For he must be your guard.
  Luc. I wish no better:
A noble gentleman, and nobly us'd me.
They call'd his name Miranda.
  Nor. You are his then: [vice.
You've lit upon a young man worth your ser-
I free you from all the rest, and from all
  violence;   [for't!
He that doth offer't, by my head, he hangs
Go see her safe kept, till the noble gentleman
Be ready to dispose her. Thank your tongue,

You have a good one, and preserve it good still.
Soldiers, come wait on me; I'll see ye paid
  all.   [*Exeunt.*

SCENE II.

Enter Miranda and Astorius.

  Asto. I knew you lov'd her, virtuously you
    lov'd her,
Which made me make that haste: I knew
  you priz'd her,
As all fair minds do goodness.
  Mir. Good Astorius,
I must confess I do much honour her,
And worthily I hope still.
  Asto. 'Tis no doubt, sir;
For on my life she's much wrong'd.
  Mir. Very likely,
And I as much tormented I was absent.
  Asto. You need not fear; Peter Gomera's
Of a tried faith and valour.   [noble,
  Mir. This I know too: [suffer'd,
But whilst I was not there, and whilst she
Whilst Virtue suffer'd, friend—Oh, how it
  loads me!   [gether—
Whilst Innocence and Sweetness sunk to-
How cold it sits here! If my arm had fought
  for her,   [sons,
My youth, tho' naked, stood against all trea-
My sword here grasp'd, Love on the edge,
  and Honour,
And but a signal from her eye to steel it [16]?
If then she had been lost—I brag too late,
And too much I decline the noble Peter.
Yet some poor service I would do her sweet-
Alas, she needs it, my Astorius;   [ness:
The gentle lady needs it.
  Asto. Noble spirit!   [this weakness!
  Mir. And what I can—'Prithee, bear with
Often I do not use these women's weapons,
But where true pity is—I am much troubled,
And something have to do, I cannot form yet!
  Asto. I'll take my leave, sir; I shall but
  disturb you.
  Mir. An't please you, for a while; and
  pray to Fortune
To smile upon this lady.
  Asto. All my help, sir.   [*Exit.*
  Mir. Gomera's old and stiff, and he may
  lose her,
The winter of his years and wounds upon him;
And yet he has done bravely hitherto:
Mountferrat's fury in his heat of summer,
The whistling of his sword like angry storms,
Renting up life by th' roots: I've seen him
As if a falcon had run up a train,   [scale
Clashing his warlike pinions, his steel'd
  cuirass,
And at his pitch inmew the town below him [17].
I must do something!

[16] *From her eye to seal it.*] To *seal a sword* seems a very odd metaphor. I think it therefore highly probable that the true word was *steel*. The propriety and elegance of which
might be proved by forty passages in Shakespear and our Authors, where it is used in the
same sense; and the reader will find it twice before the end of this act.   *Seward.*

[17] *Inmew the* town *below him.*] Theobald would read, ' the *fowl* below him;' but *scale* seems
to confirm *town.*

Enter Colonna.

Col. Noble sir, for Heav'n sake,
Take pity of a poor afflicted Christian,
Redeem'd from one affliction to another!
  Mir. Boldly you ask that; we are bound
    to give it.
From what affliction, sir?
  Col. From cold and hunger,
From nakedness and stripes.
  Mir. A prisoner?   [taken;
  Col. A slave, sir, in the Turkish prize, new
That, in the heat of fight, when your brave
    hand
Brought the Dane succour, got my irons off,
And put myself to mercy of the ocean.
  Mir. And swam to land?
  Col. I did, sir; Heav'n was gracious!
But now a stranger, and my wants upon me,
(Tho' willingly I would preserve this life, sir,
With honesty and truth) I am not look'd on;
The hand of pity, that should give for Heav'n's
    sake,
And charitable hearts, are grown so cold, sir,
Never remembring what their fortunes may
    be.
  Mir. Thou say'st too true. Of what pro-
    fession art thou?
  Col. I have been better train'd, and can
    serve truly,
Where trust is laid upon me.
  Mir. A handsome fellow!
Hast thou e'er bore arms?
  Col. I've trod full many a march, sir,
And some hurts have to shew; before me too,
    sir.
  Mir. Pity this thing should starve, or, forc'd
    for want,
Come to a worse end.—I know not what
    thou mayst be,
But if thou think'st it fit to be a servant,
I'll be a master, and a good one to thee,
If you deserve, sir.
  Col. Else I ask no favour.
  Mir. Then, sir, to try your trust, because
    I like you,
Go to the Dane; of him receive a woman,
A Turkish prisoner, for me receive her;
I hear she is my prize: Look fairly to her,
For I would have her know, tho' now my
    prisoner,   [honour.
The Christians need no schoolmasters for
Take this to buy thee cloaths; this ring, to
    help thee   [stranger,
Into the fellowship of my house; you are a
And my servants will not know you else;
    there keep her,
And with all modesty preserve your service!
  Col. A foul example find me else! Heav'n
    thank ye!
Of captain Norandine?
  Mir. The same.
  Col. 'Tis done, sir: [you!
And may Heav'n's goodness ever dwell about
  Mir. Wait there 'till I come home.
  Col. I shall not fail, sir.   [*Exeunt.*

SCENE III.

Enter Mountferrat and Abdella.

Abd. 'Tis strange it should be so, that your
    high mettle
Should check thus poorly, dully, most un-
  Mountf. Let me alone.   [manly——
  Abd. Thus leadenly——
  Mountf. Pox take you!   [dow!
  Abd. At every childish fear, at every sha-
Are you Mountferrat, that have done such
    deeds?
Wrought thro' such bloody fields men shake
    to speak of?
Can you go back? is there a safety left yet,
But fore-right? is not ruin round about you?
Have you not still these arms, that sword,
    that heart whole?
Is't not a man you fight with, and an old man,
A man half-kill'd already? am not I here?
As lovely in my black to entertain thee,
As high and full of heat to meet thy plea-
  Mountf. I'll be alone.   [sures——
  Abd. You shall: Farewell, sir!
And do it bravely! never think of conscience;
There is none to a man resolv'd. Be happy!
    [*Exit.*

Enter Miranda.

Mountf. No, most unhappy wretch, as
    thou hast made me,
More devil than thyself, I am.
  Mir. Alone,
And troubled too, I take it. How he starts!
All is not handsome in thy heart, Mount-
    ferrat.—
God speed you, sir! I have been seeking of
They say you are to fight to-day.   [you:
  Mountf. What then?
  Mir. Nay, nothing, but good fortune to
    your sword, sir!
You have a cause requires it; the island's
The order's, and your honour's.   [safety,
  Mountf. And do you make a question
I will not fight it nobly?
  Mir. You dare fight;   [justice,
You have; and with as great a confidence as
I've seen you strike as home, and hit as deadly.
  Mountf. Why are these questions then?
  Mir. I'll tell you quickly.
You have a lady in your cause, a fair one,
A gentler never trod on ground, a nobler——
  Mountf. Do you come on so fast? I have
    it for you.   [*Aside.*
  Mir. The sun ne'er saw a sweeter.
  Mountf. These I grant you;
Nor dare I against beauty heave my hand up,
It were unmanly, sir, too much unmanly:
But when these excellencies turn to ruin,
To ruin of themselves, and those protect 'em;
When virtue's lost, lust and dishonour enter'd;
Loss of ourselves and souls basely projected—
  Mir. Do you think 'tis so?
  Mountf. Too sure.
  Mir. And can it be?   [sweetness,
Can it be thought, Mountferrat, so much

So great a magazine of all things precious,
A mind so heavenly made—'Prithee observe
me.

Mountf. I thought so too: Now, by my
holy order,
He that had told me, ('till experience found it,
Too bold a proof) this lady had been vicious—
I wear no dull sword, sir, nor hate I virtue.

Mir. Against her brother? to the man has
bred her?
Her blood and honour?

Mountf. Where ambitious Lust
Desires to be above the rule prescrib'd her,
Takes hold, and wins, poor Chastity, cold
Duty,
Like fashions old forgot, she flings behind her,
And puts on blood and mischief, death and
ruin,
To raise her new-built hopes, new faith to
fasten her:
Ma'foy, she is as foul as Heav'n is beauteous!

Mir. Thou liest, thou liest, Mountferrat,
thou liest basely!
Stare not, nor swell not with thy pride! thou
liest;
And this shall make it good.

Mountf. Out with your heat first!
You shall be fought withal.

Mir. By Heav'n, that lady, deeds
The virtue of that woman, were all the good
Of all thy families bound in one faggot,
From Adam to this hour, but with one sparkle
Would fire that wisp, and turn it to light
ashes.

Mountf. Oh, pitiful young man, struck
blind with beauty! [randa!
Shot with a woman's smile! Poor, poor Mi-
Thou hopeful young man once, but now thou
lost man,
Thou naked man of all that we call noble,
How art thou cozen'd! Didst thou know what
I do,
And how far thy dear honour, (mark me, fool!)
Which like a father I have kept from blasting,
Thy tender honour, is abus'd—But fight first,
And then, too late, thou shalt know all.

Mir. Thou liest still!

Mountf. Stay! now I'll shew thee all, and
then I'll kill thee: [thee.
I love thee so dear, time shall not disgrace
Read that! [*Gives him a letter.*

Mir. It is her hand, it is most certain.
Good angels, keep me! that I should be her
agent
To betray Malta, and bring her to the basha!
That on my tender love lay all her project!
Eyes never see again, melt out for sorrow!
Did the devil do this?

Mountf. No, but his dam did it,
The virtuous lady that you love so dearly:
Come, will you fight again?

Mir. No; 'prithee kill me,
For Heav'n's sake, and for goodness' sake,
dispatch me!
For the disgrace sake that I gave thee, kill

Mountf. Why, are you guilty? [me!

Mir. I have liv'd, Mountferrat,
To see Dishonour swallow up all Virtue,
And now would die. By Heav'n's eternal
brightness,
I am as clear as Innocence!

Mountf. I knew it, [ledge,
And therefore kept this letter from all know-
And this sword from anger; you had died else.
And yet I lie, and basely lie.

Mir. Oh, Virtue,
Unspotted Virtue, whither art thou vanish'd?
What hast thou left us to abuse our frailties,
In shape of goodness?

Mountf. Come, take courage, man!
I have forgiven and forgot your rashness,
And hold you fair as light in all your actions;
And by my troth I griev'd your love. Take
comfort!
There be more women.

Mir. And more mischief in 'em!

Mountf. The justice I shall do, to right
these villainies, [sir,
Shall make you man again: I'll strike it sure,
Come, look up bravely; put this puling passion
Out of your mind. One knock for thee, Mi-
randa,
And for the boy the grave Gomera gave thee,
When she accepted thee her champion,
And in thy absence, like a valiant gentleman;
I yet remember it: ' He is too young,
' Too boyish, and too tender, to adventure:'
I'll give him one sound rap for that: I love
Thou art a brave young spark. [thee;

Mir. Boy, did he call me?
Gomera call me *boy?*

Mountf. It pleas'd his gravity, [vice,
To think so of you then: They that do ser-
And honest service, such as thou and I do,
Are either knaves or boys.

Mir. Boy, by Gomera?
How look'd he when he said it? for Gomera
Was ever wont to be a virtuous gentleman,
Humane and sweet.

Mountf. Yes, when he will, he can be.
But, let it go; I would not breed dissention;
'Tis an unfriendly office. And had it been
To any of a higher strain than you, sir [18],
The well-known, well-approv'd, and lov'd
Miranda,

---

[18] *To any of an higher strain than you are.*] At first glance, the reader may think, as I once
did with Mr. Seward, that *lighter*, or *lower*, or some such word should supply the place of
higher. But possibly the passage is right as it is, and refers only to the *even temper and dis-*
position of Miranda, and means that, had he been of an hot fiery temper prone to passion, &c.
he should not have discovered a secret, which might possibly breed dissension betwixt Gomera and him. This I only offer the reader, in order to give the text fair play: if he does not
approve of the explanation, *lighter* or *lower* are still at his service.   *Sympson.*

I had not thought on't: 'Twas happily his
    haste too,
And zeal to her.
  Mir. A traitor and a *boy* too?
Shame take me, if I suffer it!—Puff! fare-
    well, love!
  Mountf. You know my business; I must
    leave you, sir;
My hour grows on apace.
  Mir. I must not leave you,
I dare not, nor I will not, 'till your goodness
Have granted me one courtesy: You say you
    love me?
  Mountf. I do, and dearly; ask, and let
    that courtesy
Nothing concern mine honour——
  Mir. You must do it,
Or you will never see me more.
  Mountf. What is it?   [it.
It shall be great that puts you off: 'Pray speak
  Mir. 'Pray let me fight to-day, good, dear
    Mountferrat!
Let me, and bold Gomera——
  Mountf. Fy, Miranda!
D'ye weigh my worth so little?
  Mir. On my knees!
As ever thou hadst true touch of a sorrow
Thy friend conceiv'd, as ever honour lov'd
    thee——
  Mountf. Shall I turn recreant now?
  Mir. 'Tis not thy cause;
Thou hast no reputation wounded in it;
Thine's but a general zeal: 'Death! I am
    tainted;
The dearest twin to life, my credit's murder'd,
Baffled and *boy'd.*
  Mountf. I'm glad you've swallow'd it —
          [*Aside.*
I must confess I pity you; and 'tis a justice,
A great one too, you should revenge these
    injuries;
I know it, and I know you fit and bold to do't,
And man as much as man may: But, Mi-
    randa—
Why do you kneel?
  Mir. By Heav'n, I'll grow to the ground
    here,   [in't,
And with my sword dig up my grave, and fall
.Unless thou grant me—Dear Mountferrat!
    friend!
Is any thing in my power? to my life, sir!
The honour shall be yours.
  Mountf. I love you dearly;
Yet so much I should tender——
  Mir. I'll preserve all;
By Heav'n, I will, or all the sin fall with me!
'Pray let me.
  Mountf. You have won; I'll once be coward
To pleasure you.
  Mir. I kiss your hands, and thank you.
  Mountf. Be tender of my credit, and fight
    bravely.
  Mir. Blow not the fire that flames.
  Mountf. I'll send mine armour;
My man shall presently attend you with it,

(For you must arm immediately; the hour
    calls)   [cret,
I know 'twill fit you right. Be sure, and se-
And last be fortunate! farewell!—You are
    fitted:
I'm glad the load's off me.
  Mir. My best Mountferrat!   [*Exeunt.*

SCENE IV.

Enter Norandine and Doctor.

  Nor. Doctor, I'll see the combat, that's
    the truth on't;
If I had ne'er a leg, I'd crawl to see it.
  Doctor. You're most unfit, if I might coun-
    sel you,
Your wounds so many, and the air——
  Nor. The halter!
The air's as good an air, as fine an air—
Wouldst thou have me live in an oven?
  Doctor. Beside, the noise, sir;
Which, to a tender body——
  Nor. That's it, Doctor,
My body must be cur'd withal; if you'll heal
    me quickly,
Boil a drum-head in my broth; I never prosper
With knuckles o'veal, and birds in sorrel sops,
Caudles and cullices; they wash me away
Like a horse had eaten grains: If thou wilt
    cure me,
A pickled herring, and a pottle of sack, Doc-
And half a dozen trumpets!   [tor,
  Doctor. You're a strange gentleman——
  Nor. As e'er thou knew'st. Wilt thou give
    me another clister,   [lady,
That I may sit cleanly there like a French
When she goes to a masque at court? Where's
    thy hoboy?
  Doctor. I'm glad you're grown so merry.

Enter Astorius and Castriot.

  Nor. Welcome, gentlemen!
  Asto. We come to see you, sir; and glad
    we are
To see you thus, thus forward to your health,
  Nor. I thank my Doctor here.   [sir.
  Doctor. Nay, thank yourself, sir;
For, by my troth, I know not how he's cur'd!
He ne'er observes any of our prescriptions.
  Nor. Give me my money again then, good
    sweet Doctor!
Wilt thou have twenty shillings a-day for
    vexing me?
  Doctor. That shall not serve you, sir.
  Nor. Then forty shall, sir,
And that will make you speak well. Hark,
    the drums!
        [*Drums afar off: A low march.*
  Cast. They begin to beat to th' field. Oh,
    noble Dane,
Never was such a stake, I hope, of innocence,
Play'd for in Malta, and in blood, before.
  Asto. It makes us hang our heads all.
  Nor. A bold villain!
If there be treason in it—Accuse poor ladies?

And yet they may do mischief too. I'll be
   with ye:
If she be innocent I shall find it quickly,
And something then I'll say——
  Asto. Come, lean on us, sir.
  Nor. I thank ye, gentlemen! and, domine
Doctor,   [pocket,
'Pray bring a little sneezing powder in your
For fear I swoon when I see blood.
  Doctor. You're pleasant.   [*Exeunt.*

SCENE V.

Enter two Marshals.

  1 Marsh. Are the combatants come in?
  2 Marsh. Yes.
    [*The scaffold set out, and the stairs.*
  1 Marsh. Make the field clear there!
  2 Marsh. That's done too.
  1 Marsh. Then to the prisoner; the Grand-
master's coming.
Let's see that all be ready there.
  2 Marsh. Too ready.
How ceremonious our very ends are!
Alas, sweet lady, if she be innocent,
      [*Flourish.*
No doubt but justice will direct her champion.
Away! I hear 'em come.
  1 Marsh. 'Pray Heav'n she prosper!

Enter Valetta, Norandine, Astorius, Castriot,
    &c.

  Val. Give captain Norandine a chair.
  Nor. I thank your lordship.
  Val. Sit, sir, and take your ease; your
  hurts require it:
You come to see a woman's cause decided;
(That's all the knowledge now, or name, I've
  for her)
They say a false, a base, and treach'rous wo-
And partly prov'd too.   [man,
  Nor. Pity it should be so;
And, if your lordship durst ask my opinion,
Sure I should answer No, (so much I honour
  her)
And answer't with my life too. But Gomera
Is a brave gentleman; the other valiant,
And if he be not, good, dogs gnaw his flesh
  off!
And one above 'em both will find the truth
He never fails, sir.   [out;
  Val. That's the hope rests with me.
  Nor. How nature and his honour struggle
  in him!
A sweet, clear, noble gentleman!
  [*Guard within.*] Make room there!

Enter Oriana, Ladies, Executioner, Abdella,
   and Guard.

  Val. Go up, and what you have to say,
  say there.
  Ori. Thus I ascend; nearer, I hope, to
Heav'n!

Nor do I fear to tread this dark black man-
  sion,
The image of my grave; each foot we move
Goes to it still, each hour we leave behind us
Knolls sadly toward it. My noble brother,
(For yet mine innocence dares call you so)
And you the friends to virtue, that come hi-
  ther,
The chorus to this tragick scene, behold me,
Behold me with your justice, not with pity,
(My cause was ne'er so poor to ask compas-
  sion)
Behold me in this spotless white I wear,
The emblem of my life, of all my actions;
So ye shall find my story, tho' I perish.
Behold me in my sex; I am no soldier;
Tender and full of fears our blushing sex is,
Unharden'd with relentless thoughts; un-
  hatcht [19]   [tremble
With blood and bloody practice: Alas, we
But when an angry dream afflicts our fancies,
Die with a tale well told. Had I been prac-
  tis'd,   [it,
And known the way of mischief, travell'd in
And giv'n my blood and honour up to reach it;
Forgot religion, and the line I sprung on;
Oh, Heav'n! I had been fit then for thy jus-
  tice,   [here.
And then in black, as dark as hell, I'd howl'd
Last, in your own opinions weigh mine inno-
  cence:
Amongst ye I was planted from an infant,
('Would then, if Heav'n had so been pleas'd,
  I'd perish'd!)
Grew up, and goodly, ready to bear fruit,
The honourable fruit of marriage:
And am I blasted in my bud, with treason?
Boldly and basely of my fair name ravish'd,
And hither brought to find my rest in ruin?
But he that knows all, he that rights all
  wrongs,   [spoken.
And in his time restores, knows me!—I've
  Val. If ye be innocent, Heav'n will pro-
  tect ye,
And so I leave ye to his sword strikes for ye;
Farewell!   [brother,
  Ori. Oh, that went deep! Farewell, dear
And howsoe'er my cause goes, see my body
(Upon my knees I ask it) buried chastely;
For yet, by holy truth, it never trespass'd.
  Asto. Justice sit on your cause, and Heav'n
  fight for ye!   [honour
  Nor. Two of ye, gentlemen, do me but the
To lead me to her; good my lord, your leave
  Val. You have it, sir.   [too.
  Nor. Give me your fair hands fearless:
As white as this I see your innocence,
As spotless, and as pure; be not afraid, lady!
You are but here brought to your nobler
  fortune,
To add unto your life immortal story:
Virtue thro' hardest things arrives at happi-
  ness.

---

[19] See note 56 on The Custom of the Country.   *Sympson.*

Shame follow that blunt sword that loses you!
And he that strikes against you, I shall study
A curse or two for him. Once more, your
　　fair hands!
I ne'er brought ill luck yet; be fearless, hap-
　Ori. I thank ye, noble captain.　[py.
　Nor. So I leave ye.
　Val. Call in the knights severally.

　　Enter severally, Gomera and Miranda.

　Ori. But two words to my champion;
And then to Heav'n and him I give my cause
　Val. Speak quickly, and speak short. [up.
　Ori. I have not much, sir.
Noble Gomera, from your own free virtue
You've undertaken here a poor maid's honour,
And with the hazard of your life; and happily
You may suspect the cause, tho' in your true
　　worth　　　　　　　　[timony,
You will not shew it; therefore take this tes-
(And, as I hope for happiness, a true one!)
And may it steel your heart, and edge your
　　good sword!
You fight for her, as spotless of these mischiefs
As Heav'n is of our sins, or Truth of errors;
And so defy that treacherous man, and pro-
　Nor. Blessing o' thy heart, lady! [sper!
　Val. Give the signal to 'em. [Low alarms.
　Nor. 'Tis bravely fought! Gomera, follow
　　that blow—
Well struck again, boy!—look upon the lady,
And gather spirit! brave again! lie close,
Lie close, I say! he fights aloft, and strongly;
Close for thy life!—A pox o' that fell buffet!
Retire and gather breath; ye've day enough,
　　knights—
Look lovely on him, lady! to't again now!
Stand, stand, Gomera, stand—one blow for
　　all now!　　　　　　[woman!
Gather thy strength together; God bless the
Why, where's thy noble heart? Heav'n bless
，　the lady!
　All. Oh, oh!
　Val. She is gone, she is gone.
　Nor. Now strike it.
Hold, hold—he yields: Hold thy brave sword,
　　he's conquer'd—
He's thine, Gomera. Now be joyful, lady!
What could this thief have done, had his
　　cause been equal!
He made my heart-strings tremble.
　Val. Off with's casque there [20];
And, executioner, take you his head next.
　Abd. Oh, cursed Fortune!　　[Aside.

　Gom. Stay, I beseech you, sir! and this
　　one honour
Grant me, I have deserv'd it; that this villain
May live one day, to envy at my justice;
That he may pine and die, before the sword
　　fall,
Viewing the glory I have won, her goodness.
　Val. He shall; and you the harvest of your
　　valour
Shall reap, brave sir, abundantly.
　Gom. I've sav'd her,　　　[struction [21],
Preserv'd her spotless worth from black de-
(Her white name to eternity deliver'd)　[in.
Her youth and sweetness from a timeless ru-
Now, lord Valetta, if this bloody labour
May but deserve her favour——
　Mir. Stay, and hear me first.
　Val. Off with his casque! This is Miran-
　　da's voice.
　Nor. 'Tis he indeed, or else mine eyes
　　abuse me:
What makes he here thus?
　Ori. The young Miranda?
Is he mine enemy too?
　Mir. None has deserv'd her,
If worth must carry it, and service seek her,
But he that sav'd her honour.
　Gom. That is I, Miranda.　　[forward!
　Mir. No, no; that's I, Gomera; be not so
In bargain for my love you cannot cozen me.
　Gom. I fought it.
　Mir. And I gave it, which is nobler.
Why, every gentleman would have done as
　　much　　　　　　　　[sir;
As you did: Fought it? that's a poor desert,
They're bound to that. But then to make
　　that fight sure,
To do as I did, take all danger from it,
Suffer that coldness that must call me now
·Into disgrace for ever, into pity——
　Gom. I undertook first, to preserve her
　　from hazard.
　Mir. And I made sure no hazard should
　　come near her.
　Gom. 'Twas I defied Mountferrat.
　Mir. 'Twas I wrought him,
(You'd had a dark day else) 'twas I defied
His conscience first, 'twas I that shook him
Which is the brave defiance.　　[there,
　Gom. My life and honour
At stake I laid.
　Mir. My care and truth lay by it,
Lest that stake might be lost. I have de-
　　serv'd her,

---

[20] Cask.] This word is generally spelt *casque*. It signifies here *a helmet*, and sometimes is used only for *a beaver*, or *hat*.　R.
　[21] *Preserv'd her spotless worth from black* destruction.] If by *worth* the Poets mean her *worthy self*, to save that from destruction, would be only saying the same thing, with pre-serving　　　'Her youth, and sweetness, from a timeless ruin,'
three lines below. But if by *worth* be meant her *fame* and *character*, I then should think *destruction* a corruption, and would propose reading the line so:
　　　'Preserv'd her spotless worth from black *detraction*.'　Sympson.
　Detraction would be best, were there authority for the change.

And none but I: The lady might have pe-
rish'd   [malice,
Had fell Mountferrat struck it, from whose
With cunning and bold confidence, I catch'd
it;
And 'twas high time. And such a service,
lady,   .   [knows
For you, and for your innocence—for who
Not th' all-devouring sword of fierce Mount-
ferrat?   [spiteful,
I shew'd you what I could do, had I been
Or master but of half the poison he bears:
(Hell take his heart for't!) And beshrew
these hands, madam,
With all my heart, I wish a mischief on 'em!
They made you once look sad: Such another
fright
I would not put you in, to own the island:
Yet, pardon me; 'twas but to shew a soldier,
Which when I'd done, I ended your poor
coward.
Val. Let some look out, for the base knight
Mountferrat——   [trusty.
Abd. I hope he's far enough, if his man be
This was a strange misfortune; I must not
know it.
Val. That most deboshed knight. Come
down, sweet sister,
My spotless sister now! 'Pray thank these
gentlemen;
They have deserv'd both truly, nobly of you,
Both excellently, dearly, both all the honour,
All the respect and favour— —
Ori. Both shall have it;
And as my life their memories I'll nourish.
Val. Ye're both true knights, and both
most worthy lovers;
Here stands a lady ripen'd with your service,
Young, fair, and (now I dare say) truly ho-
nourable:
'Tis my will she shall marry, marry now,
And one of you (she cannot take more nobly):
Your deserts
Begot this will, and bred it. Both her beauty
Cannot enjoy; dare you make me your um-
Gom. Mir. With all our souls.   [pire?
Val. He must not then be angry
That loses her.
Gom. Oh, that were, sir, unworthy.
Mir. A little sorrow he may find.
Val. 'Tis manly.   [man;
Gomera, you're a brave accomplish'd gentle-
A braver no where lives than is Miranda.
In the white way of virtue, and true valour,
You've been a pilgrim long; yet no man fur-
ther
Has trod those thorny steps than young Mi-
randa:

You're gentle, he is gentleness itself: Ex-
perience
Calls you her brother; this her hopeful heir.
Nor. The young man now, an't be thy will!
Val. Your hand, sir!
You undertook first, nobly undertook,
This lady's cause; you made it good, and
fought it;   [her!
You must be serv'd first, take her and enjoy
I give her to you: Kiss her! Are you pleas'd
now?
Gom. My joy's so much I cannot speak.
Val. Nay, fairest sir,   [promise.
You must not be displeas'd; you break your
Mir. I never griev'd at good; nor dare I
now, sir,
Tho' something seem strange to me.
Val. I've provided
A better match for you, more full of beauty;
I'll wed you to our order: There's a mistress
Whose beauty ne'er decays (Time stands be-
low her);
Whose honour, ermin-like, can never suffer
Spot or black soil; whose eternal issue
Fame brings up at her breasts, and leaves 'em
Her you shall marry.   [sainted;
Mir. I must humbly thank you.
Val. Saint Thomas' Fort, a charge of no
small value,
I give you too, in present, to keep waking
Your noble spirits; and, to breed you pious,
I'll send you a probation-robe; wear that,
'Till you shall please to be our brother.—
How now?

Enter Astorius.

Asto. Mountferrat's fled, sir.
Val. Let him go a while,   [coupled:
'Till we have done these rites, and seen these
His mischief now lies open. Come, all
friends now!
And so let's march to th' temple. Sound
those instruments,
That were the signal to a day of blood!
Evil beginning hours may end in good.
[*Flourish.*
Nor. Come, we'll have wenches, man, and
all brave things.
Pox! let her go; we'll want no mistresses;
Good swords, and good strong armours!
Mir. Those are best, captain.
Nor. And fight 'till queens be in love with
us, and run after us.
I'll see you at the fort within these two days;
And let's be merry, 'prithee!
Mir. By that time I shall.
Nor. Why, that's well said! I like a good
heart truly.   [*Exeunt.*

ACT III.

SCENE I.

Enter Norandine and Servant, Corporal and Soldiers above.

Serv. THE day is not yet broke, sir.
　　Nor. 'Tis the cooler riding.
I must go see Miranda: Bring my horse
Round to the South port; I'll out here at the beach,
And meet you at the end o' th' sycamores:
'Tis a sweet walk, and if the wind be stirring
Serves like a fan to cool.
　　Serv. Which walk?
　　Nor. Why, that, sir.
Where the fine city-dames meet to make matches.
　　Serv. I know it. [*Exit. Singing above.*
　　Nor. Speed ye then [22] !—What mirth is this?
The watches are not yet discharg'd, I take it:
These are brave careless rogues! I'll hear the song out,
And then I'll fit ye for't, merry companions!

SONG, *by the Soldiers.*

1. Sit, soldiers, sit and sing, the round is clear,
　And cock-a-loodle-looe tells us the day is near. [mellow,
　Each toss his cann, until his throat be
　Drink, laugh, and sing; the soldier has no fellow!

2. To thee a full pot, my little lance-prisado,
　And when thou hast done, a pipe of Trinidado!
　Our glass of life runs wine, the vintner skinks it [23],
　Whilst with his wife the frolick soldier drinks it.

3. The drums beat, ensigns wave, and cannons thump it;
　Our game is ruffe, and the best heart doth trump it: [low,
　Each toss his cann, until his throat be mel-
　Drink, laugh, and sing; the soldier has no fellow!

4. I'll pledge thee, my Corporal, were it a flagon; [dragon;
　After, watch fiercer than George did the
　What blood we lose i' th' town, we gain i' th' tuns;
　Furr'd gowns, and flat caps, give the wall to guns. [low,
　Each toss his cann, until his throat be mel-
　Drink, laugh, and sing; the soldier has no fellow.

Nor. Here's notable order! Now for a trick to tame ye!
Owgh, owgh!
　1 *Watch.* Hark, hark! what's that below us? Who goes there?
　Nor. Owgh, owgh, owgh!
　2 *Watch.* 'Tis a bear broke loose; 'pray call the Corporal.
　1 *Watch.* The Dutchman's huge fat sow.
　2 *Watch.* I see her now,
And five fine pigs.
　Nor. Owgh, owgh!

Enter Corporal.

Corp. Now, what's the matter? [ral,
　1 *Watch.* Here's the great fat sow, Corpo-
The Dutchman's sow; and all the pigs, brave fat pigs:
You have been wishing long, she would break
　Nor. Owgh, owgh! [loose.
Corp. 'Tis she indeed; there's a white pig now sucking:
Look, look! d'you see it, sirs?
　1 *Watch.* Yes, very well, sir.
Corp. A notable fat whoreson! Come, two of ye,
Go down with me; we'll have a tickling break-
　2 *Watch.* Let's eat 'em at the Cross. [fast.
Corp. There's the best liquor.
　Nor. I'll liquor some of ye, ye lazy rogues!
Your minds are of nothing but eating and swilling.
What a sweet beast they've made of me! A
Hog upon hog! I hear 'em come. [sow?

Enter Corporal below, and Watch.

Corp. Go softly,
And fall upon 'em finely, nimbly.
　1 *Watch.* Bless me!
Corp. Why, what's the matter?
　1 *Watch.* Oh, the devil! the devil,
As high as a steeple!
　2 *Watch.* There he goes, Corporal!
His feet are cloven too.
Corp. Stand, stand, I say! [kets?
Death, how I shake! Where be your mus-
　1 *Watch.* There's
No good of them: Where be our prayers, man?
　2 *Watch.* Lord, how he stalks! speak to him, Corporal.
Corp. Why, what a devil art thou?
　Nor. Owgh, owgh!
Corp. A dumb devil?

---

[22] *Nor. Speed ye then, &c.*] This and the three following lines have hitherto been placed *after* the Song, which they should undoubtedly *precede.* It is not printed in the first folio.

[23] *The vintner skinks it.*] As we can affix no idea to the word *slinks* here, we have substituted *skinks.* A *skinker,* the very ingenious Dr. Percy tells us, is ' one that serves drink.' The word occurs as late as Dryden's Translation of the First Book of Homer.

The worst devil that could come, a dumb
  devil!
Give me a musket. He gathers in to me!
I' th' name of——Speak! what art thou?
  Speak, devil, or
I'll put a plumb in your belly.
  Nor. Owgh, owgh, owgh!
  Corp. Fy, fy! in what a sweat I am! Lord
  bless me,
My musket's gone too! I am not able to stir it.
  Nor. Who goes there? Stand, speak!
  Corp. Sure I am enchanted!
Yet here's my halbert still. Nay, who goes
  there, sir?
What, have I lost myself? What are ye?
  Nor. The guard.
  Corp. Why, what are we then? He's not
  half so long now,
Nor h'has no tail at all. I shake still dam-
  Nor. The word! [nably.
  Corp. Have mercy on me! what word does
  he mean?
'Prithee, devil, if thou be'st the devil, do not
Make an ass of me! for I remember yet,
As well as I am here, I am the Corporal;
I'll lay my life on't, devil.
  Nor. Thou art damn'd! [Corporal?
  Corp. That's all one; but am not I the
I'd give a thousand pound to be resolv'd now.
Had not I soldiers here?
  Nor. No, not a man;
Thou art debosh'd, and cozen'd,
  Corp. That may be, [been?
It may be I am drunk.—Lord, where have I
Is not this my halbert in my hand?
  Nor. No, 'tis a May-pole.
  Corp. Why then, I know not who I am,
  nor what,
Nor whence I come.
  Nor. You are an arrant rascal!
You corporal of a watch?
  Corp. 'Tis the Dane's voice. You are no
  devil then?
  Nor. No, nor no sow, sir. [ne'er
  Corp. Of that I am right glad, sir; I was
So frighted in my life, as I am a soldier.
  Nor. Tall watchmen! [centries:
A guard for a goose! you sing away your
A careful company! Let me out o' the port
  here,
(I was a little merry with your worships)
And keep your guards strong, tho' the devil
  walk.

Hold, there's to bring ye into your wits again.
Go off no more to hunt pigs; such another
And you will hunt the gallows. [trick,
  Corp. 'Pray, sir, pardon us!
And, let the devil come next, I'll make him
Or make him stink. [stand,
  Nor. Do, do your duty truly.
Come, let me out, and come away [54].
                     [*Exeunt.*

SCENE II.

Enter Abdella with a letter, and Rocca.

  Rocca. No more rage.
  Abd. Write thus to me? H'hath fearfully
  and basely
Betray'd his own cause; yet, to free himself,
He now ascribes the fault to me.
  Rocca. I know not
What he hath done; but what he now desires
His letters have inform'd you.
  Abd. Yes; he is
Too well acquainted with the power he holds
Over my mad affections!—I want time
To write; but 'pray you tell him, if I were
No better steel'd in my strong resolution
Than he hath shewn himself in his, or th..... bt
There was a hell hereafter, or a Heaven
But in enjoying him, I should stick here,
And move no further. Bid him yet take com-
  fort; [at,
For something I will do the devil would quake
But I'll untie this nuptial knot of love,
And make way for his wishes. In the mean
  time
Let him lie close, (for he is strictly sought for)
And practise to love her, that for his ends
Scorns fear and danger!

Enter Oriana and Velleda.

  Rocca. All this I will tell him. [*Exit.*
  Abd. Do so. Farewell!—My lady, with
  my fellow,
So earnest in discourse!—Whate'er it be,
I'll second it.
  Vel. He's such a noble husband,
In every circumstance so truly loving,
That I might say, and without flattery, ma-
The sun sees not a lady but yourself [dam,
That can deserve him.
  Abd. Of all men, I say,
That dare (for 'tis a desperate adventure)
Wear on their free necks the sweet yoke of
  woman,

---

[54] *Come, let me out, and come away; no more ruge.*

SCENE II.

Enter Abdella with a letter, and Rocca.

  Abd. Write thus to me?] If this latter part of the line belong to Norandine, 'tis strangely
odd; for why must he say *no more ruge?* This implies, that the corporal and the guard had
been in one before, which the reader knows is so far from true, that they were frighted with
the mimic grunt of a hog, and took it for the devil; but supposing Abdella had been storming
at Mountferrat's letter, some time before Rocca's and her coming upon the stage, these
mollifying words of his to her, viz. *no more rage,* will be exceedingly in character, and highly
proper to introduce the angry speech of Abdella. *Sympson.*

(For they that do repine are no true husbands)
Give me a soldier!
Ori. Why? are they more loving
Than other men?
Abd. And love too with more judgement:
For, but observe, your courtier is more curious
To set himself forth richly, than his lady;
His baths, perfumes, nay paintings too, more
costly
Than his frugality will allow to her;
His cloaths as chargeable; and grant him but
A thing without a beard, and he may pass
At all times for a woman, and with some
Have better welcome: Now, your man of
lands
For the most part is careful to manure them,
But leaves his lady fallow; your great mer-
chant
Breaks oftner for the debt he owes his wife,
Than with his creditors; and that's the reason
She looks elsewhere for payment: Now, your
Vel. Ay, marry, do him right! [soldier—
Abd. First, who has one
Has a perpetual guard upon her honour;
For while he wears a sword, Slander herself
Dares not bark at it; next, she sits at home
Like a great queen, and sends him forth to
fetch in
Her tribute from all parts; which, being
brought home,
He lays it at her feet, and seeks no further
For his reward than what she may give freely,
And with delight too, from her own exchequer,
Which she finds ever open.
Ori. Be more modest!
Abd. Why, we may speak of that we're
glad to taste of,
Among ourselves I mean.
Ori. Thou talk'st of nothing.
Abd. Of nothing, madam? You have found
it something;
Or, with the raising-up this pretty mount
My lord hath dealt with spirits.   [here,

Enter Gomera.

Ori. Two long hours absent?
Gom. Thy pardon, sweet! I have been
looking on   [Dane,
The prize that was brought in by the brave
The valiant Norandine, and have brought
something
That may be thou wilt like of; but one kiss,
And then possess my purchase: There's a
piece   -
Of cloth of tissue, this of purple velvet,
And (as they swear) of the right Tyrian dye,
Which others here but weakly counterfeit:
If they are worth thy use, wear them; if not,
Bestow them on thy women.
Abd. Here's the husband!   [sea,
Gom. While there is any trading on the
Thou shalt want nothing. 'Tis a soldier's
However he neglect himself, to keep [glory,
His mistress in full lustre.

Ori. You exceed, sir.
Gom. Yet there was one part of the prize
dispos'd of
Before I came, which I grieve that I miss'd of,
Being almost assur'd, it would have been
A welcome present.
Ori. 'Pray you say, what was it?
Gom. A Turkish captive, of incomparable
beauty,
And, without question, in her country noble;
Which, as companion to thy faithful Moor,
I would have given thee for thy slave.
Ori. But was she
Of such an exquisite form?
Gom. Most exquisite.
Ori. And well descended?
Gom. So the habit promis'd,
In which she was ta'en.
Ori. Of what years?
Gom. 'Tis said
A virgin of fourteen.
Ori. I pity her,
And wish she were mine, that I might ha'
the means
To entertain her gently.
Gom. She is now Miranda's;
And, as I've heard, made it her suit to be so.
Ori. Miranda's? then her fate deserves
not pity,
But envy rather.
Gom. Envy, Oriana?
Ori. Yes, and their envy that live free.
Gom. How's this?   [one,
Ori. Why, she is fallen into the hands of
So full of that which in men we stile Good-
ness,
That, in her being his slave, she's happier far
Than if she were confirm'd the sultan's mis-
tress.
Gom. Miranda is indeed a gentleman
Of fair desert, and better hopes; but yet
He hath his equals.
Ori. Where? I would go far,
As I am now, tho' much unfit for travels,
But to see one that without injury
Might be put in the scale, or parallel'd,
In any thing that's noble, with Miranda.
His knowledge in all services of war,
And ready courage to put into act
That knowing judgment, as you are a soldier,
You best may speak of; nor can you deliver,
Nor I hear with delight, a better subject.
And Heav'n did well, in such a lovely feature
To place so chaste a mind; for he is of
So sweet a carriage, such a winning nature,
And such a bold, yet well-dispos'd behaviour;
And, to all these, h'has such a charming
tongue,   [colours,
That, if he would serve under Love's fresh
What monumental trophies might he raise
Of his free conquests, made in ladies' favours!
Gom. Yet you did resist him, when he was
An earnest suitor to you?
Ori. Yes, I did;

And, if I were again sought to, I should;
But must ascribe it rather to the fate
That did appoint me yours, than any power
Which I can call mine own.

Gom. E'en so?

Abd. Thanks, Fortune!
The plot I had to raise in him doubts of her
Thou hast effected.

Ori. I could tell you too,
What cause I have to love him; with what reason
In thankfulness he may expect from me
All due observance; but I pass that, as
A benefit for which, in my behalf,
You are his debtor.

Abd. I perceive it takes,
By his chang'd looks.

Ori. He is not in the city,
Is he, my lord?

Gom. Who, lady?

Ori. Why, Miranda:
Having you here, can there be any else
Worth my enquiry?

Gom. This is somewhat more   [*Aside.*
Than love to virtue!

Ori. 'Faith, when he comes hither,
(As sometimes, without question, you shall meet him)
Invite him home.

Gom. To what end?

Ori. To dine with us,
Or sup.   [you;

Gom. And then to take a hard bed with
Mean you not so?

Ori. If you could win him to it,
'Twould be the better. For his entertainment,
Leave that to me; he shall find noble usage,
And from me a free welcome.

Gom. Have you never
Heard of a Roman lady, Oriana,
Remember'd as a precedent for matrons,
(Chaste ones. I pray you understand) whose husband,
Tax'd for his sour breath by his enemy,
Condemn'd his wife for not acquainting him
With his infirmity?

Ori. 'Tis a common one:
Her answer was, having kiss'd none but him,
She thought it was a general disease
All men were subject to. But what infer you
From that, my lord?

Gom. Why, that this virtuous lady
Had all her thoughts so fix'd upon her lord,
That she could find no spare time to sing praises
Of any other; nor would she employ
Her husband (tho' perhaps in debt to years
As far as I am) for an instrument
To bring home younger men, that might delight her
With their discourse, or——

Ori. What, my lord?

Gom. Their persons;
Or, if I should speak plainer——

Ori. No, it needs not;

You've said enough to make my innocence
It is suspected.   [know

Gom. You betray yourself
To more than a suspicion: Could you else,
To me, that live in nothing but love to you,
Make such a gross discov'ry, that your lust
Had sold that heart, I thought mine, to Miranda?
Or rise to such a height in impudence,
As to presume to work my yielding weakness
To play, for your bad ends, to my disgrace,
The wittol, or the pander?

Ori. Do not study   [ny]
To print more wounds (for that were tyran-
Upon a heart that is pierc'd thro' already.

Gom. Thy heart? thou hast pierc'd thro'
mine honour, false one,
The honour of my house! Fool that I was,
To give it up to the deceiving trust   [ture,
Of wicked woman! For thy sake, vile crea-
For all I have done well in, in my life,
I've digg'd a grave, all buried in a wife;
For thee I have defied my constant mistress,
That never fail'd her servant, glorious War;
For thee refus'd the fellowship of an order
Which princes, thro' all dangers, have been
To fetch as far as from Jerusalem: [proud
And am I thus rewarded?

Vel. By all goodness,
You wrong my lady, and deserve her not,
When you are at your best! Repeat your
'Twill shew well in you.   [rashness;

Abd. Do, and ask her pardon.

Ori. No; I have liv'd too long, to have
my faith,   [him
My tried faith, call'd in question, and by
That should know true affection is too tender
To suffer an unkind touch, without ruin.
Study ingratitude, all, from my example!
For to be thankful now is to be false.
But, be't so; let me die! I see you wish it;
Yet dead, for truth and pities' sake, report
What weapon you made choice of when you
kill'd me.

Vel. She faints!

Abd. What have you done?

Ori. My last breath cannot
Be better spent, than to say I forgive you;
Nor is my death untimely, since with me
I take along what might have been hereafter
In scorn deliver'd for the doubtful issue
Of a suspected mother.   [*She swoons.*

Vel. Oh, she's gone!

Abd. For ever gone!—Are you a man?

Gom. I grow here!

Abd. Open her mouth, and pour this cor-
dial in it:
If any spark of life be unquench'd in her,
This will recover her.

Vel. 'Tis all in vain!
She's stiff already. Live I, and she dead?

Gom. How like a murderer I stand!—
Look up,
And hear me curse myself, or but behold
The vengeance I will take for't, Oriana,

And then in peace forsake me! Jealousy,
Thou loathsome vomit of the fiends below,
What desp'rate hunger made me to receive
thee
Into my heart, and soul? I'll let thee forth,
And so in death find ease! And does my
fault then   [live
Deserve no greater punishment? No; I'll
To keep thee for a fury to torment me,
And make me know what hell is on the earth!
All joys and hopes forsake me! all men's
malice,
And all the plagues they can inflict, I wish it,
Fall thick upon me! let my tears be laugh'd at,
And may mine enemies smile to hear me
groan;
And, dead, may I be pitied of none!
                                         [*Exeunt.*

SCENE III.

Enter Colonna and Lucinda.

Luc. 'Pray you, sir, why was the ordnance
of the fort
Discharg'd so suddenly?
Col. 'Twas the governor's pleasure,
In honour of the Dane; a custom us'd,
To speak a soldier's welcome.
Luc. 'Tis a fit one.
But is my master here too?
Col. Three days since.   [much,
Luc. Might I demand without offence so
Is't pride in him (however now a slave)
That I am not admitted to his presence?
Col. His courtesy to you, and to mankind,
May easily resolve you, he is free
From that poor vice which only empty men
Esteem a virtue.
Luc. What's the reason then,
As you imagine, sir?
Col. Why, I will tell you:
You are a woman of a tempting beauty,
And he, however virtuous, as a man,
Subject to human frailties; and how far
They may prevail upon him, should he see
you,
He is not ignorant; and therefore chuses
With care t'avoid the cause that may produce
Some strange effect, which will not well keep
rank
With the rare temperance which is admir'd
In his life hitherto.
Luc. This much encreases
My strong desire to see him.
Col. It should rather   [worship,
Teach you to thank the prophet that you
That you are such a man's, who, tho' he may

Do any thing which youth and heat of blood
Invites him to, yet dares not give way to them.
Your entertainment's noble, and not like
Your present fortune; and (if all those tears
Which made grief lovely in you, i'th' relation
Of the sad story that forc'd me to weep too,
Your husband's hard fate, were not counter-
feit)   [pay
You should rejoice that you have means to
A chaste life to his memory, and bring to him
Those sweets, which while he liv'd he could
not taste of:
But if you wantonly bestow them on
Another man, you offer violence   [suffer
To him, tho' dead; and his griev'd spirit will
For your immodest looseness.
Luc. Why, I hope, sir,
My willingness to look on him to whom
I owe my life and service, is no proof
Of any unchaste purpose.
Col. So I wish too!
And in the confidence it is not, lady,
I dare the better tell you he will see you
This night, in which by him I am commanded
To bring you to his chamber; to what end
I easily should guess, were I Lucinda [25]:
And therefore, tho' I can yield little reason
(But in a general love to women's goodness)
Why I should be so tender of your honour,
I willingly would bestow some counsel of you;
And would you follow it?
Luc. Let me first hear it,
And then I can resolve you.
Col. My advice then
Is, that you would not (as most ladies use,
When they prepare themselves for such en-
counters)
Study to add, by artificial dressings,
To native excellence; yours, without help,
But seen as it is now, would make a hermit
Leave his death's head, and change his after-
hopes
Of endless comforts, for a few short minutes
Of present pleasures; to prevent which, lady,
Practise to take away from your perfections,
And to preserve your chastity unstain'd:
The most deform'd shape that you can put on,
To cloud your body's fair gifts, or your mind's,
(It being labour'd to so chaste an end)
Will prove the fairest ornament.
Luc. To take from
The workmanship of Heaven is an offence
As great as to endeavour to add to it;
Of which I'll not be guilty.   Chastity,
That lodges in deformity, appears rather
A mulct impos'd by Nature, than a blessing;
And 'tis commendable only when it conquers,

---

[25] ——— *to what end*
I easily should guess, were I Miranda;] Before we condemn this *Miranda*, let us put the
sense of this passage into plain prose. You are intended to be brought into Miranda's chamber this night, says Colonna to Lucinda, and if I was *Miranda*, I could easily guess for what
end, &c. *i. e.* if I sent for you, I could surely tell why I sent for you. Is not this mighty
elegant? I doubt not but my reader sees where the fault lies, and has made the correction
for me: '*I easily should guess, was I Lucinda.*'   Sympson.

Tho' ne'er so oft assaulted, in resistance:
For me, I'll therefore so dispose myself,
That if I hold out it shall be with honour;
Or if I yield, Miranda shall find something
To make him love his victory. [*Exit.*

Col. With what cunning
This woman argues for her own damnation!
Nor should I hold it for a miracle,
Since they are all born sophisters, to maintain
That lust is lawful, and the end and use
Of their creation. 'Would I never had
Hop'd better of her, or could not believe,
Tho' seen, the ruin I must ever grieve! [*Exit.*

SCENE IV.

*Enter Miranda, Norandine, Servants with
lights.*

Mir. I'll see you in your chamber.
Nor. 'Pray you no further!
It is a ceremony I expect not:
I am no stranger here; I know my lodging,
And have slept soundly there, when the Turks'
cannon
Play'd thick upon it: Oh, 'twas royal musick!
And to procure a sound sleep for a soldier,
Worth forty of your fiddles. As you love me,
Press it no further!
Mir. You will overcome.—
Wait on him carefully.
Nor. I've took, since supper,
A rouse or two too much[26], and, by the gods,
It warms my blood.
Mir. You'll sleep the better for't.
Nor. Pox on't, I should, had but I a kind
wench [cap,
To pull my boot-hose off, and warm my night-
There's no charm like it. I love old Adam's
way; [time!
Give me a diligent Eve, to wait towards bed-
Hang up your smooth-chin page! And, now
I think on't,
Where is your Turkish prisoner?
Mir. In the castle;
But yet I never saw her.
Nor. Fy upon you!

See her, for shame! or, hark you; if you
would [part,
Perform the friend's part to me, the friend's
It being a fashion of the last edition,
Far from panderism, now send her to me.
You look strange on't[27]! No entertainment's
perfect
Without it, on my word, no livery like it!
I'll tell her he looks for it as duly
As for his fee.—There's no suit got without it;
Gold is an ass to't.
Mir. Go to bed, to bed!
Nor. Well, if she come, I doubt not to
convert her;
If not, the sin lie on your head!—Good night!
[*Exeunt Nor. and Servants.*

Enter Colonna and Lucinda.

Col. There you shall find him, lady: You
know what I've said,
And if you please you may make use.
Luc. No doubt, sir.
Col. From hence I shall bear all.
[*He retires.*
Mir. Come hither, young one.—
Beshrew my heart, a handsome wench!—
Come nearer.
A very handsome one!—Do not you grieve,
You are a prisoner? [sweet,
Luc. The loss of liberty,
No doubt, sir, is a heavy and sharp burden
To them that feel it truly: But your servant,
Your humble handmaid, never felt that rigour;
Thanks to that noble will! No want, no
hunger
(Companions still to slaves), no violence,
Nor any unbeseeming act we start at,
Have I yet met withal: Content and goodness,
Civility, and sweetness of behaviour,
Dwell round about me; therefore, worthy
master,
I cannot say I grieve my liberty. [dier,
Mir. Do not you fancy me too cold a sol-
Too obstinate an enemy to youth,
That had so fair a jewel in my cabinet,
And in so long a time would ne'er look on it?

[26] *A rouse.*] This seems in general to signify what we now call *a cheerful glass.*—It is a
word which frequently occurs, but not always in the same sense: 'Fore Heaven, they have
given me a *rouse* already,' says Cassio in Othello, act iii. scene 3, and Mr. Steevens says,
that ' a *rouse* appears to be a quantity of liquor rather too large;' and, in proof of it, cites
Hamlet and the following passage in The Christian Turned Turk, 1612:
'—— our friends may tell
' We drank a *rouse* to them.'
But neither this passage nor that in the text warrants Steevens's explanation:—*A* rouse *or*
two TOO MUCH implies that a *rouse* is not in itself too much, no more than if we were to say
a *glass* or two too much.
[27] Nor. *You look strange on't, no entertainment's perfect*
Without it, on my word, no livery like it;]
The passage ' I'll tell her he looks for it as duly
' As for his fee ——'
which I have recovered from the folio of the oldest date, is not to be found in the succeeding
editions; but I must confess I don't understand the latter part of the speech, any more
than I know reason why the editors of the copies of 1679 and 1711 thought proper to
drop it. *Sympson.*
The passage seems corrupt; or, at least, not to belong to this place.

Col. What can she say now?

Luc. Sure, I desir'd to see you;
And with a longing wish——

Col. There's all her virtue.

Luc. Pursued that full desire, to give you
    thanks, sir,
The only sacrifice I've left, and service,
For all the virtuous care you've kept me safe

Col She holds well yet.   [with.

Mir. The pretty fool speaks finely.—
Come, sit down here.

Luc. Oh, sir, 'tis most unseemly.

Mir. I'll have it so; sit close Now tell me
Did you e'er love yet?   [truly,

Luc. My tears will answer that, sir [a].

Mir. And did you then love truly?

Luc. So I thought, sir.

Mir. Can you love me so?

Col. Now!

Luc. With all my duty;
I were unworthy of those favours else,
You daily shower upon me.

Mir. What think'st thou of me?

Luc. I think you are a truly worthy gentle-
    man,
A pattern, and a pride, to the age you live in,
Sweet as the commendations all men give you.

Mir. A pretty flatt'ring rogue!—Dare you
    kiss that sweet man
You speak so sweetly of? Come.

Col. Farewell, virtue!

Mir. What hast thou got between thy lips?
    (Kiss once more)
Sure thou hast a spell there!

Luc. More than e'er I knew, sir.

Col. All hopes go now!

Mir. I must tell you
A thing in your ear; and you must hear me,
And hear me willingly, and grant me so too;
'Twill not be worth my asking else.

Luc. It must be
A very hard thing, sir, and from my power,
I shall deny your goodness.

Mir. 'Tis a good wench!—
I must lie with you, lady.

Luc. 'Tis something strange;
For yet in all my life I knew no bedfellow.

Mir. You'll quickly find that knowledge.

Luc. To what end, sir?

Mir. Art thou so innocent thou canst not
    guess at it?
Did thy dreams ne'er direct thee?

Luc. 'Faith, none yet, sir.

Mir. I'll tell thee then: I would meet thy
    youth, and pleasure;
Give thee my youth for that, (by Heav'n, she
    fires me!)
And teach thy fair white arms, like wanton
A thousand new embraces.   [ivies,

Luc. Is that all, sir?
And say I should try, may not we lie quietly?
Upon my conscience, I could!

Mir. That's as we make it.

Luc. Grant that that likes you best, what
    would you do then?   [baby,

Mir. What would I do? Certainly I'm no
Nor brought up for a nun. Hark in thine ear!

Luc. Fy, fy, sir!

Mir. I would get a brave boy on thee,
A warlike boy.

Luc. Sure we shall get ill Christians.

Mir. We'll mend 'em in the breeding then.

Luc. Sweet master!

Col. Never belief in woman come near
    me more!   [virgin

Luc. My best and noblest sir, if a poor
(For yet, by Heaven, I'm so) should chance
    so far
(Seeing your excellence, and able sweetness)
To forget herself, and slip into your bosom,
Or to your bed, out of a doting on you,
(Take it the best way) have you that cruel
That murd'ring mind, to——   [heart,

Mir. Yes, by my troth, sweet, have I,
To lie with her.

Luc. And do you think it well done?

Mir. That's as she'll think when 'tis done.
    Come to bed, wench!
For thou'rt so pretty, and so witty a com-
We must not part to-night.   [panion,

Luc. 'Faith, let me go,
Sir, and think better on't.

Mir. I'faith, thou shalt not!
I warrant thee, I'll think on't.

Luc. I've heard 'em say here,
You are a maid too.

Mir. I am sure I am, wench,
If that will please thee.

Luc. I have seen a wonder!   [ness,
And would you lose that, for a little wanton-
(Consider, my sweet master, like a man, now)
For a few honied kisses, slight embraces,
That glory of your youth? that crown of
    sweetness
Can you deliver? that unvalued treasure
Would you forsake, to seek your own dis-
    honour?
What gone, no age recovers, nor repentance?
To a poor stranger?

Col. Hold there, again thou'rt perfect!

Luc. I know you do but try me,

Mir. And I know   [bed!
I'll try you a great deal further. 'Prithee, to
I love thee, and so well—Come, kiss me once
    more!
Is a maidenhead ill bestow'd o' me?

Luc. What's this, sir?
        [*Taking hold of his cross.*

Mir. Why, 'tis the badge, my sweet, of
    that holy order
I shortly must receive, the Cross of Malta.

Luc. What virtue has it?

Mir. All that we call virtuous.

Luc. Who gave it first?

Mir. He that gave all, to save us.

Luc. Why then, 'tis holy too?

[a] *My years will answer that, sir.*] Corrected from Sympson's conjecture.

Mir. True sign of holiness;
The badge of all his soldiers that profess him.
　　Luc. The badge of all his soldiers that pro-
　　fess him?
Can it save in dangers?
　　Mir. Yes.
　　Luc. In troubles, comfort?
　　Mir. You say true, sweet.
　　Luc. In sickness, restore health?
　　Mir. All this it can do.
　　Luc. Preserve from evils that afflict our
　　frailties?
　　Mir. I hope she will be Christian.—All
　　these truly.
　　Luc. Why are you sick then, sick to death
　　with lust?
In danger to be lost? no holy thought　[ties,
In all that heart? Nothing but wandring frail-
Wild as the wind, and blind as death or ig-
Inhabit there.　　　　　　　　　[norance,
　　Mir. Forgive me, Heav'n! she says true.
　　Luc. Dare you profess that badge, pro-
　　phane that goodness——
　　Col. Thou hast redeem'd thyself again,
　　most rarely!
　　Luc. That holiness and truth you make me
　　wonder at?
Blast all the bounty Heav'n gives? that re-
　　membrance—

　　Col. Oh, excellent woman!
　　Luc. Fling it from you quickly,
If you be thus resolv'd; I see a virtue
Appear in't like a sword, both edges flaming,
That will consume you, and your thoughts,
　　to ashes.
Let them profess it that are pure, and noble,
Gentle, and just of thought, that build the
　　Cross,
Not those that break it! By Heaven, if you
　　touch me,　　　　　　　　　　[you.
Ev'n in the act, I'll make that Cross, and curse
　　Mir. You shall not, fair: I did dissemble
　　with you,
And but to try your faith I fashion'd all this.
Yet something you provok'd me. This fair
　　Cross,
By me (if he but please to help first gave it)
Shall ne'er be worn upon a heart corrupted.
Go to your rest, my modest, honest servant,
My fair and virtuous maid, and sleep secure
　　there;
For when you suffer, I forget this sign here.
　　Col. A man of men too! Oh, most perfect
　　gentleman!　　　　　　　　　[Christian.
　　Luc. All sweet rest to you, sir! I'm half a
The other half I'll pray for; then for you, sir.
　　Mir. This is the foulest play I'll shew.
　　Good night, sweet!　　　　　　[*Exeunt.*

ACT IV.

SCENE I.

Enter Mountferrat and Rocca.

Mountf. THE sun's not set yet?
　　Rocca. No, sir.
　　Mountf. 'Would it were,
Never to rise again to light the world!
And yet, to what vain purpose do I wish it,
Since, tho' I were environ'd with thick mists,
Black as Cymerian darkness, or my crimes,
There is that here, upon which, as an anvil,
Ten thousand hammers strike, and every
　　spark,
They force from it, to me's another sun
To light me to my shame?
　　Rocca. Take hope and comfort.
　　Mountf. They're aids indeed, but yet as
　　far from me
As I from being innocent. This cave, fashion'd
By provident Nature in this solid rock,
To be a den for beasts, alone receives me;
And having prov'd an enemy to mankind,
All human helps forsake me.
　　Rocca. I'll ne'er leave you;　　[courage,
And wish you would call back that noble
That old invincible fortitude of yours,
That us'd to shrink at nothing.
　　Mountf. Then it did not;　　[height
But 'twas when I was honest! Then, i' th'
Of all my happiness, of all my glories,

Of all delights that made life precious to me,
I durst die, Rocca! Death itself then to me
Was nothing terrible, because I knew
The fame of a good knight would ever live
Fresh on my memory: But since I fell
From my integrity, and dismiss'd those guards,
Those strong assurances of innocence;
That constancy fled from me; and, what's
　　worse,
Now I am loathsome to myself, and life
A burden to me; rack'd with sad remem-
　　brance
Of what I have done, and my present horrors
Unsufferable to me; tortur'd with despair
That I shall ne'er find mercy; hell about me,
Behind me, and before me; yet I dare not,
Still fearing worse, put off my wretched being!

　　Enter Abdella.

　　Rocca. To see this would deter a doubtful
　　man　　　　　　　　　　　　[practice
From mischievous intents, much more the
Of what is wicked. Here's the Moor; look
Some ease may come from her.　　[up, sir!
　　Mountf. New trouble rather,
And I expect it.
　　Abd. Who is this? Mountferrat?
Rise up, for shame! and, like a river dried up
With a long drought, from me, your boun-
　　teous sea,

Receive those tides of comfort that flow to
If ever I look'd lovely; if desert   [you.
Could ever challenge welcome; if revenge,
And unexpected wreak, were ever pleasing,
Or could endear the giver of such blessings;
All these I come adorn'd with, and, as due,
Make challenge of those so-long-wish'd em-
          braces,
Which you, unkind, have hitherto denied me.
  Mountf. Why, what have you done for
  Abd. Made Gomera   [me?
As truly miserable, as you thought him happy:
Could you wish more?
  Mountf. As if his sickness could
Recover me! The injuries I receiv'd
Were Oriana's.
  Abd. She has paid dear for 'em;
She's dead.
  Mountf. How!   [ther.
  Abd. Dead; my hate could reach no fur-
Taking advantage of her in a swoon,
Under pretence to give a cordial to her,
I poison'd her.—What stupid dullness is this?
What you should entertain with sacrifice,
Can you receive so coldly?
  Mountf. Bloody deeds
Are grateful offerings, pleasing to the devil;
And thou, in thy black shape, and blacker
   actions,
Being hell's perfect character, art delighted
To do what I, tho' infinitely wicked,
Tremble to hear. Thou hast, in this, ta'en
   from me
All means to make amends, with penitence,
To her wrong'd virtues, and despoil'd me of
The poor remainder of that hope was left me,
For all I have already, or must suffer.
  Abd. I did it for the best.
  Mountf. For thy worst ends!
And be assur'd, but that I think to kill thee
Would but prevent what thy despair must
   force thee
To do unto thyself, and so to add to
Thy most assur'd damnation, thou wert dead
   now.
But, get thee from my sight! and if lust of me
Did ever fire thee (love I cannot call it)
Leap down from those steep rocks, or take
   advantage
Of the next tree to hang thyself, and then
I may laugh at it.
  Abd. In the mean time, I must
Be bold to do so much for you: Ha, ha!
  Mountf. Why grin'st thou, devil?
  Abd. That 'tis in my power
To punish thy ingratitude. I made trial
But how you stood affected, and since I
Know I'm us'd only for a property,
I can and will revenge it to the full:
For understand, in thy contempt of me,
Those hopes of Oriana, which I could
Have chang'd to certainties, are lost for ever.

  Mountf. Why, lives she?
  Abd. Yes; but never to Mountferrat,
Altho' it is in me, with as much ease
To give her freely up to thy possession,
As to remove this rush; which yet despair of:
For, by my much-wrong'd love, flattery, nor
   threats,
Tears, prayers, nor vows, shall ever win me
So, with my curse, I leave thee!   [to it:
  Mountf. 'Prithee, stay!
Thou know'st I dote on thee, and yet thou art
So peevish, and perverse, so apt to take
Trifles unkindly from me——
  Abd. To persuade me   [self,
To break my neck, to hang, then damn my-
With you are trifles!
  Mountf. 'Twas my melancholy   [give!
That made me speak I know not what: For-
I will redeem my fault.
  Rocca. Believe him, lady.
  Mountf. A thousand times I will demand
   thy pardon,   [kisses.
And keep the reckoning on thy lips with
  Abd. There's something else, that would
   prevail more with me.
  Mountf. Thou shalt have all thy wishes:
   Do but bless me
With means to satisfy my mad desires
For once in Oriana, and for ever
I am thine, only thine, my best Abdella!
  Abd. Were I assur'd of this, and that you
Having enjoy'd her——   [would,
  Mountf. Any thing! make choice of
Thine own conditions.
  Abd. Swear then, that perform'd,
(To free me from all doubts and fears here-
To give me leave to kill her.   [after)
  Mountf. That our safety
Must of necessity urge us to.
  Abd. Then know,
It was not poison, but a sleeping potion,
Which she receiv'd; yet of sufficient strength
So to bind up her senses, that no sign
Of life appear'd in her; and thus thought
In her best habit [99], as the custom is   [dead,
(You know) in Malta, with all ceremonies
She's buried in her family's monument,
I' th' temple of St. John: I'll bring you thither,
Thus, as you are disguis'd. Some six hours
The potion will leave working.   [hence
  Rocca. Let us haste then.
  Mountf. Be my good angel; guide me!
  Abd. But remember
You keep your oath.
  Mountf. As I desire to prosper
In what I undertake!
  Abd. I ask no more.   [*Exeunt.*

SCENE II.

Enter Miranda, Norandine, and Colonna.

  Col. Here, sir; I've got the key: I bor-
   row'd it

---

[99] *In her best habit,* &c.] This speech bears an obvious similitude to one of Friar Laurence in Shakespeare's Romeo and Juliet.

Of him that keeps the church; the door is
open.

Mir. Look to the horses then, and please
the fellow,
After a few devotions, I'll retire.
Be not far off; there may be some use of you.
Give me the light. Come, friend, a few good
prayers   •
Were not bestow'd in vain now, e'en from
you, sir: ['em,
Men that are bred in blood, have no way left
No bath, no purge, no time to wear it out
Or wash it off, but penitence and prayer.
I am to take the order; and my youth
Loaden, I must confess, with many follies,
Circled and bound about with sins as many
As in the house of memory live figures.
My heart I'll open now, my faults confess,
And rise a new man, Heav'n, I hope, to a new
life.   [stant;
Nor. I have no great devotion, at this in-
But, for a prayer or two, I will not out, sir.
Hold up your finger when you've pray'd
Mir. Go you to that end.   [enough.
Nor. I shall never pray
Alone sure, I have been so us'd to answer
The clerk. 'Would I had a cushion; for I
Shall ne'er make a good hermit, and kneel 'till
My knees are horn; these stones are plaguy
hard!
Where shall I begin now? for if I do not
Observe a method, I shall be out presently.
Ori. Oh, oh!
Nor. What's that, sir? Did you hear?
Mir. Ha? to your prayers!
Nor. 'Twas hereabouts! It has put me
clean awry
Now; I shall ne'er get in again! Ha! by land,
And water, all children and all women;
Ay, there it was I left.
Ori. Oh, oh!
Nor. Ne'er tell me, sir!
Here's something got amongst us.
Mir. I heard a groan,
A dismal one.
Ori. Oh, oh!
Nor. Here, 'tis here, sir, 'tis here, sir!
A devil in the wall!
Mir. 'Tis some illusion
To fright us from devotion.
Ori. Oh, oh!
Nor. Why, 'tis here;
The spirit of a huntsman choak'd with butter[30].
Here's a new tomb, new trickments too.
Mir. For certain,
This has not been three days here.
Nor. And a tablet
With rhimes upon't.
Mir. I prithee read 'em, Norandine.
Nor. An epi—an epi—taph, I think 'tis;
ay, 'tis taph!

An epitaph upon the most excel—excel—
lent—and—
Mir. Thou canst not read.   [der.
Nor. I've spoil'd mine eyes with gunpow-
Mir. An epitaph upon the most virtuous
and excellent lady,
The honour of chastity, Oriana.
Nor. The Grand-master's sister? how a
devil came she here?
When slipt she out o' th' way? The stone's
but half upon her.   [mischief
Mir. It is a sudden change!—Certain the
Mountferrat offer'd to her broke her heart-
strings.
Nor. 'Would he were here! I'd be the
clerk myself,
And, by this little light, I'd bury him alive
Here's no lamenting now.   •   [here.
Ori. Oh, oh!
Nor. There 'tis.
Mir. Sure from   [her.
The monument! the very stone groans for
Oh, dear lady, blessing of women, virtue of
thy sex;
How art thou set for ever, how stol'n from us!
Babbling and prating now converse with wo-
Nor. Sir, it rises; it looks up!   [men.
                              [*She rises up.*
Mir. Heav'n bless us!   [higher.
Nor. it is in woman's cloaths. It rises
Mir. It looks about, and wonders: Sure
she lives, sir!
'Tis she, 'tis Oriana, 'tis that lady.
Nor. Shall I go to her?
Ori. Where am I?
Mir. Stand still.
Ori. What place is this?
Nor. She is as live as I am.
Ori. What smell of earth, and rotten bones?
what dark place?
Lord, whither am I carried?
Nor. How she stares,
And sets her eyes upon him!
Mir. How is't, dear lady?
D' you know me? how she shakes!
Ori. You are a man.
Mir. A man that honours you.
Ori. A cruel man;
Ye are all cruel! Are you in your grave too?
For there's no trusting cruel man, above
Nor. By'r lady, that goes hard! [ground.
Mir. To do you service,
And to restore you to the joys you were in—
Ori. I was in joys indeed, and hope——
Mir. She sinks again?
Again she's gone, she's gone, gone as a sha-
She sinks for ever, friend!   [dow!
Nor. She is cold now;
She's certainly departed: I must cry too.
Mir. The blessed angels guide thee! Put
the stone to.

---

[30] *The spirit of a* huntsman *choak'd with butter.*] As I can see no humour in a *huntsman's*
being choak'd with butter, I make no doubt of its being a corruption for *Dutchman,* who are
always laughed at for eating such quantities of oiled butter.   *Seward.*

Beauty, thou'rt gone to dust, goodness to
     ashes!
Nor. 'Pray take it well; we must all have
     our hours, sir.   [glory
Mir. Ay, thus we are; and all our painted
A bubble that a boy blows into the air,
And there it breaks.
Nor. I am glad you sav'd her honour yet.
Mir. 'Would I had sav'd her life now too!
     Oh, Heav'n,
For such a blessing, such a timely blessing!
Oh, friend, what dear content 'twould be,
     what story
To keep my name from worms!
Ori. Oh, oh!
Nor. She lives again!
'Twas but a trance.
Mir. 'Pray you call my man in presently.
Help with the stone first! Oh, she stirs again!
Oh, call my man! away!
Nor. I fly, I fly, sir!   [*Exit.*
Mir. Upon my knees, oh, Heav'n, oh,
     Heav'n, I thank thee!

Enter Colonna and Norandine.

The living heat steals into every member.
Come, help the coffin out softly, and sud-
Where is the clerk?   [denly!
Col. Drunk above; he is sure, sir.
Mir. Sirrah, you must be secret.
Col. As your soul, sir.
Mir. Softly, good friend! take her into
     your arms.
Nor. Put in the crust again.
Mir. And bring her out there. When I
     am a-horse-back,
My man and I will tenderly conduct her
Unto the fort; stay you, and watch what issue,
And what enquiry's for the body.
Nor. Well, sir?   [me.
Mir. And when you've done, come back to
Nor. I will.
Mir. Softly, oh, softly!
Nor. She grows warmer still, sir.
Col. What shall I do with the key?
Mir. Thou canst not stir now;
Leave it i' th' door. Go, get the horses ready.
                                       [*Exeunt.*

*Enter Rocca, Mountferrat, and Abdella
     with a dark-lanthorn.*

Rocca. The door's already open, the key in
Mountf. What were those past by?   [it.
Rocca. Some scout of soldiers, I think.
Mountf. It may be well so, for I saw their
They saw not us, I hope.   [horses:
Abd. No, no, we were close;
Beside, they were far off.
Mountf. What time of night is't?
Abd. Much about twelve, I think.
Rocca. Let me go in first;
For, by the leaving open of the door here,
There may be somebody i' th' church. Give
me the lanthorn.
Abd. You'll love me now, I hope.

Mountf. Make that good to me
Your promise is engag'd for.
Abd. Why, she's there,
Ready prepar'd; and much about this time
Life will look up again.
Rocca. Come in; all's sure;
Not a foot stirring, nor a tongue.
Mountf. Heav'n bless me!
I never enter'd, with such unholy thoughts,
This place before.
Abd. You are a fearful fool!
If men have appetites allowed 'em,   ['em?
And warm desires, are there not ends too for
Mountf. Whither shall we carry her?
Rocca. Why, to the bark, sir;
I have provided one already waits us:
The wind stands wondrous fair too for our
     passage.
Abd. And there, when you've enjoy'd her,
     (for you've that liberty)
Let me alone to send her to feed fishes!
I'll no more sighs for her.
Mountf. Where is the monument?
Thou'rt sure she will awake about this time?
Abd. Most sure,
If she be not knockt o' th' head. Give me
     the lanthorn!
Here 'tis.—How's this? the stone off?
Rocca. Ay, and nothing
Within the monument, that's worse; no body,
I'm sure of that, nor sign of any here,
But an empty coffin.
Mountf. No lady?
Rocca. No, nor lord, sir;
This pie has been cut up before.
Abd. Either the devil
Must do these tricks——
Mountf. Or thou, damned one, worse!
Thou black swoln pitchy cloud of all my af-
     flictions,   [suffer'd,
Thou night-hag, gotten when the bright moon
Thou hell itself confin'd in flesh, what trick
     now?
Tell me, and tell me quickly, what thy mis-
     chief   [whither
Has done with her, and to what end, and
Thou hast remov'd her body; or, by this
     holy place,
This sword shall cut thee into thousand pieces,
A thousand thousand, strew thee o'er the tem-
     ple,
A sacrifice to thy black sire, the devil!
Rocca. Tell him; you see he's angry.
Abd. Let him burst!
Neither his sword nor anger do I shake at;
Nor will yield, to feed his poor suspicions,
His idle jealousies, and mad-dogs' heats,
One thought against myself. You've done a
     brave deed,
A manly, and a valiant piece of service,
When you have kill'd me! reckon't amongst
     your battles!   [man,
I'm sorry you're so poor, so weak a gentle-
Able to stand no fortune: I dispose of her?
My mischief make her away? a likely project,

I must play booty 'gainst myself! If any thing
  cross ye,
I am the devil, and the devil's heir;
All plagues, all mischiefs——
  Mountf. Will you leave, and do yet?
  Abd. I have done too much,
Far, far too much, for such a thankless fellow!
If I be devil, you created me:
I never knew those arts, nor bloody practices,
(Plague o' your cunning heart, that mine of
  mischief!)
Before your flatteries won 'em into me.—
Here did I leave her, leave her with that cer-
About this hour to wake again.   [tainty
  Mountf. Where is she?
This is the last demand.
  Abd. Did I now know it,
And were I sure this were my latest minute,
I would not tell thee: Strike, and then I'll
  curse thee.
  Rocca. I see a light. Stand close, and
  leave your angers!
We all miscarry else.

    Enter Gomera, and Page with a torch.

  Abd. I am now careless.
  Mountf. Peace, 'prithee peace, sweet!
  peace! all friends!
  Abd. Stand close then.
  Gom. Wait there, boy, with the light, 'till
  I call to thee.
In darkness was my soul and senses clouded
When my fair jewel fell, the night of jealousy
In all her blackness drawn about my judg-
  ment;
No light was let into me, to distinguish
Betwixt my sudden anger and her honour:
A blind sad pilgrimage shall be my penance;
No comfort of the day will I look up at;
Far darker than my jealous ignorance,
Each place of my abode shall be; my prayers
No ceremonious lights shall set off more;
Bright arms, and all that carry lustre, life,
Society, and solace, I forsake ye!
And were it not once more to see her beauties,
(For, in her bed of death, she must be sweet
  still)
And on her cold sad lips seal my repentance,
Thou child of Heav'n, fair Light, I could not
  miss thee³¹.
  Mountf. I know the tongue: 'Would I
  were out again!
I've done him too much wrong to look upon
  him.
  Abd. There is no shifting now; boldness
  and confidence

Must carry't now away: He's but one neither,
Naked as you are, of a strength far under.
  Mountf. But h' has a cause above me!
  Abd. That's as you handle it.
  Rocca. Peace! he may go again, and ne-
  ver see us.
  Gom. I feel I weep apace; but where's the
  flood,   [in?
The torrent of my tears, to drown my fault
I would I could now, like a loaden cloud,
Begotten in the moist South, drop to nothing!
Give me the torch, boy.
  Rocca. Now he must discover us.
  Abd. He has already.—Never hide your
  head;   [ther——
Be bold and brave! If we must die, toge-
  Gom. Who's there? what friend to sor-
  row?—The tomb wide open!
The stone off too? the body gone, by Heaven!
Look to the door, boy! keep it fast!—Who
  are ye?   [ferrat,
What sacrilegious villains?—False Mount-
The wolf to honour! has thy hellish hunger
Brought thee to tear the body out o' th' tomb
  too?
Has thy foul mind so far wrought on thee?—
  Ha!
Are you there too? Nay, then I spy a villainy
I never dream'd of yet. Thou sinful usher,
Bred from that rottenness, thou bawd to
  mischief,
D' you blush thro' all your blackness? won't
  that hide it?
  Abd. I cannot speak.
  Gom. You're well met, with your dam, sir.
Art thou a knight? did ever on that sword
The Christian cause sit nobly? could that
  hand fight,
Guided by fame and fortune? that heart in-
  flame thee,
With virtuous fires of valour? To fall off,
Fall off so suddenly, and with such foulness,
As the false angels did, from all their glory!
Thou art no knight! Honour thou never
  heard'st of,
Nor brave desires could ever build in that
  breast!   [gods
Treason, and tainted thoughts, are all the
Thou worship'st, all the strength thou hast,
  and fortune!   [villain,
Thou didst things out of fear, and false heart,
Out of close traps and treach'ries; they have
  rais'd thee
  Mountf. Thou rav'st, old man.
  Gom. Before thou get'st off from me.
Hadst thou the glory of thy first fights on thee,

---

³¹ *Thou child of Heav'n, fair light, I could not miss thee.*] Seward proposes to read, 'I
'would not use thee;' and Sympson says, 'What Gomera intends to say is only this; that
'unless it was to see the beauty of his (supposed) dead wife, &c. he never should *desire* or
'*want light more.* Now this by an easy change may be made out thus:
    '———— fair light, I *should* not miss thee.'
But neither Sympson nor Seward seems to have observed, that the whole speech turns on
Gomera's abandoning *light* for darkness, which is the only key to explain the last line; but,
adverting to that, it becomes intelligible. Sympson explains the passage quite wrong.

(Which thou hast basely lost) thy noblest
    fortunes,   [thee,
And in their greatest lustres, I would make
Before we part, confess (nay, kneel, and do it,
Nay, crying kneel, coldly, for mercy, crying)
Thou art the recreant'st rogue time ever
    nourish'd;
Thou art a dog, I'll make thee swear, a dog [32],
A mangy cur dog! D' you creep behind the
    altar?
Look, how it sweats, to shelter such a rascal!
First, with thy venomous tooth infect her
    chaste life,
And then not dare to do? next, rob her rest,
Steal her dead body out o' th' grave——
    Mountf. I have not.
    Gom. 'Prithee, come out; (this is no place
      to quarrel in)
Valiant Mountferrat, come!
    Mountf. I will not stir.
    Gom. Thou hast thy sword about thee,
That good sword that ne'er fail'd thee : 'Pri-
    thee come !   [boy!
We'll have but five strokes for it. On, on,
Here is one would fain be acquainted with
    thee,
Would wondrous fain cleave that calf's head
    of yours, sir :
Come, 'prithee let's dispatch ! the moon shines
    finely :   [else;
'Prithee, be kill'd by me ! thou wilt be hang'd
But, it may be, thou longest to be hang'd.
    Rocca. Out with him, sir !
You shall have my sword too; when he's
    dispatch'd once,
We have the world before us.
    Gom. Wilt thou walk, fellow?
I never knew a rogue hang arse-ward so,
And such a desperate knave too.
    Abd. 'Pray go with him !
Something I'll promise too
    Mountf. You would be kill'd then ?
No remedy, I see.
    Gom. If thou dar'st do it?
    Mountf. Yes, now I dare. Lead out; I'll
    follow presently;
Under the mount I'll meet you.
    Gom. Go before me ;
I'll have you in a string too.
    Mountf. As I'm a gentleman,
And by this holy place, I will not fail thee.
Fear not, thou shalt be kill'd, take my word
I will not fail.   [for it;
    Gom. If thou scap'st, thou hast cats' luck.
The mount?
    Mountf. The same. Make haste, I'm
    there before else.

    Gom. Go, get ye home. Now if he scape,
    I'm coward.
    Mount. Well, now I am resolv'd ; and he
    shall find it.   [*Exeunt.*

SCENE III.

Enter Miranda, Lucinda, and Colonna.

    Mir. How is it with the lady?
    Luc. Sir, as well
As it can be with one, who feeling knows now
What is the curse the divine justice laid
On the first sinful woman.
    Mir. Is she in travail?   [mind
    Luc. Yes, sir; and yet the troubles of her
Afflict her more than what her body suffers ;
For, in the extremity of her pain, she cries
    out,
' Why am I here? where is my lord Gomera?'
Then sometimes names Miranda, and then
    sighs,
As if to speak, what questionless she loves
If heard, might do her injury.   [well,
    Col. Heaven's sweet mercy
Look gently on her !
    Mir. 'Prithee tell her, my prayers [vide
Are present with her ; and, good wench, pro-
That she want nothing ! What's thy name?
    Luc. Lucinda.   [in it !
    Mir. Lucinda? there's a prosperous omen
Be a Lucina to her, and bring word
That she is safe deliver'd of her burden,
And thy reward's thy liberty. Come, Colonna,
We will go see how th' engineer has mounted
The cannon the Great-master sent. Be careful
To view the works, and learn the discipline
That is us'd here ! I am to leave the world ;
And for your service, which I have found
    faithful,
The charge that's mine, if I have any power,
Hereafter may concern you.
    Col. I still find
A noble master in you.
    Mir. 'Tis but justice;
Thou dost deserve it in thy care and duty.
               [*Exeunt.*

SCENE IV.

Enter Gomera, Mountferrat, Rocca, and
         Abdella.

    Gom. Here's even ground; I'll stir no foot
    beyond it.
Before I have thy head.
    Mountf. Draw, Rocca !
    Gom. Coward,   [rage
Hath inward guilt robb'd thee as well of cou-

---

[32] *Thou art a dog, I'll make thee swear, a dog.*] The first folio copy has an addition to
this verse, which is wrote there thus :
        ' I'll make thee swear a dog *stav'd.*'
But what business *stav'd* has here I cannot discover; a *stav'd* dog in the bear-garden lan-
guage, I believe, is no more than a dog taken off the bear, by wrenching his mouth open to
make him leave his hold. Possibly the Poets might have wrote it thus : ' a dog *starv'd*,' and
then ' a mangy cur dog' may follow agreeably enough.   *Sympson.*

As honesty, that without odds thou dar'st not
Answer a single enemy?
Mountf. All advantage
That I can take, expect.
Rocca. We know you're valiant;
Nor do we purpose to make further trial
Of what you can do now, but to dispatch you.
Mountf. And therefore fight and pray
   together.
Gom. Villains,   [one
Whose baseness all disgraceful words made
Cannot express! so strong is the good cause
That seconds me, that you shall feel, with
   horror
To your proud hopes, what strength is in
   that arm,   [justice.
Tho' old, that holds a sword made sharp by
Abd. You come then here to prate?
       [Fight.
Mountf. Help, Rocca, now,
Or I am lost for ever!—How comes this?
       [He is disarm'd.
Are villainy and weakness twins?
Rocca. I'm gone too.
Gom. You shall not scape me, wretches!
Abd. I must do it;
All will go wrong else.   [Shoots him.
Gom. Treach'rous, bloody woman,
What hast thou done?
Abd. Done a poor woman's part,
And in an instant, what these men so long
Stood fooling for.
Mountf. This aid was unexpected;
I kiss thee for't.
Rocca. His right arm's only shot,
And that compell'd him to forsake his sword;
He's else unwounded.
Mountf. Cut his throat!
Abd. Forbear!—
Yet do not hope 'tis with intent to save thee,
But that thou mayst live to thy further tor-
   ment,   [ferrat,
To see who triumphs o'er thee. Come, Mount-
Here join thy foot to mine, and let our hearts
Meet with our hands! The contract that is
   made
And cemented with blood, as this of ours is,
Is a more holy sanction, and much surer,
Than all the superstitious ceremonies
You Christians use.

Enter Norandine.

Rocca. Who's this?
Mountf. Betray'd again?
Nor. By the report it made, and by the wind,
The pistol was discharg'd here.
Gom. Norandine,
As ever thou lov'dst valour, or wear'st arms
To punish baseness, shew it!
Nor. Oh, the devil!   [Beauty,
Gomera wounded, and my brache [33], Black
An actor in it?
Abd. If thou strik'st, I'll shoot thee.
Nor. How! fright me with your pot-gun?
   —What art thou?
Good Heav'n, the rogue, the traitor rogue,
   Mountferrat!
To swinge the nest of you, is a sport unlook'd
Hell's plagues consume you!   [for.
Mountf. As thou art a man,
(I'm wounded) give me time to answer thee!
Gom. Durst thou urge this? this hand can
   hold a sword yet.
Nor. Well done! to see this villain makes
   my hurts
Bleed fresh again; but had I not a bone whole,
In such a cause I should do thus, thus, rascals!

Enter Corporal and Watch.

Corp. Disarm them, and shoot any that
   resists.
Gom. Hold, Corporal! I am Gomera.
Nor. 'Tis well yet, that once in an age
   you can
Remember what you watch for: I had thought
You had again been making out your parties
For sucking pigs: 'Tis well. As you will
   answer
The contrary with your lives, see these forth-
Corp. That we shall do.   [coming!
Nor. You bleed apace. Good soldiers,
Go help him to a surgeon.
Rocca. Dare the worst [34],
And suffer like yourself.
Abd. From me learn courage.
Nor. Now for Miranda! this news will be
   to him
As welcome as 'tis unexpected. Corporal,
There's something for thy care to-night. My
   horse there!   [Exeunt.

---

[33] Brache.] 'Brache,' says bishop Warburton (note on Othello, act ii. scene 1,) 'is a low
'species of *hounds of the chase,* and a term generally used in contempt. Vlitius in his notes
'on Gratius says, *Racha* Saxonibus canem significabat, unde Scoti hodie *Racke* pro cane
'femina habent, quod Anglis est *Brache.* Nos verò (he speaks of the Hollanders) *Brach*
'non quemvis canem sed sagacem vocamus. So the French, *Braque,* espece de chien de
'chasse.' R.

[34] Rocca. *Dare the worst.*] I suspect a speech of Mountferrat's is dropt upon us, here,
and perhaps the reader may be of my opinion. *Sympson.*
Surely, no; Mountferrat's party have been talking apart, to be sure. J. N.

ACT V.

SCENE I.

Enter Oriana and Lucinda.

Ori. HOW does my boy ?

    Luc. Oh, wondrous lusty, madam ;
A little knight already : You shall live
To see him toss a Turk,

    Ori. Gentle Lucinda,   [*vice ;*
Much must I thank thee for thy care and ser-

Enter Miranda, Norandine, and Colonna.

And may I grow but strong to see Valetta ※,
My husband, and my brother, thou shalt find
I will not barely thank thee.

    Mir. Look, captain, we must ride away
        this morning :
The Auberge sits to-day, and the Great-mas-
Writes plainly, I must or deliver in   [ter
(The year expir'd) my probation-weed,
Or take the cloak. You likewise, Norandine,
For your full service, and your last assistance
In false Mountferrat's apprehension,
Are here commanded to associate me,
My twin in this high honour.

    Nor. I will none on't !
Do they think to bind me to live chaste, sober,
And temperately, all days of my life ?   [so !
They may as soon tie an Englishman to live
I shall be a sweet Dane, a sweet captain,
Go up and down drinking small-beer, and
swearing,   [still ;
'Ods neagues ! No ; I'll live a squire at arms
And do thou so too, an thou be'st wise.
I've found the mystery now, why the gentle-
men
Wear but three bars of the cross, and the
The whole one.   [knights

    Mir. Why, captain ?

    Nor. Marry, sir,
To put us in remembrance, we are but
Three quarters cross'd in our licence and
pleasures ;
But the poor knights cross'd altogether.
The brothers at arms may yet meet with
    their sisters at arms,   [knights
Now and then, in brotherly love ; but the poor
Cannot get a lady for love nor money :
'Tis not so in other countries, I wis. 'Pray
haste you !
For I'll along, and see what will come on't.
        [*Exit.*

    Mir. Colonna, provide straight all neces-
saries
For this remove, the litter for the lady,

And let Lucinda bear her company !
You shall attend on me.

    Col. With all my duties.   [*Exit.*

    Mir. How fare you, gracious mistress ?

    Ori. Oh, Miranda,
You pleas'd to honour me with that fair title
When I was free, and could dispose myself ;
But now, no smile, no word, no look, no
Can I impart to any, but as theft   [touch,
From my Gomera ; and who dares accept
Is an usurper.

    Mir. Leave us.—I have touch'd thee,
        [*Exit Luc.*
Thou fairer virtue, than thou'rt beautiful !—
Hold but this test, so rich an ore was never
Tried by the hand of man, on the vast earth.—
Sit, brightest Oriana ! Is it sin
Still to profess I love you, still to vow
I shall do ever ? Heav'n my witness be,
'Tis not your eye, your cheek, your tongue,
no part
That superficially doth snare young men,
Which has caught me ! Read over in your
thoughts
The story that this man hath made of you,
And think upon his merit.

    Ori. Only thought
Can comprehend it !

    Mir. And can you be
So cruel, thankless, to destroy his youth
That sav'd your honour, gave you double life,
Your own, and your fair infant's ? that when
Fortune
(The blind foe to all beauty, that is good)
Bandied you from one hazard to another,
Was even Heaven's messenger, by Providence
Call'd to the temple, to receive you there
Into these arms, to give ease to your throws,
As if 't had thunder'd ; take thy due, Miranda ;
For she was thine ! Gomera's jealousy
Struck death unto thy heart ; to him be dead,
And live to me, that gave thee second life !
Let me but now enjoy thee ! Oh, regard
The torturing fires of my affections !

    Ori. Oh, master them, Miranda, as I mine !
Who follows his desires, such tyrants serves
As will oppress him insupportably.
My flames, Miranda, rise as high as thine,
For I did love thee 'fore my marriage ;
Yet would I now consent, or could I think
Thou wert in earnest, (which, by all the souls
That have for chastity been sanctified,
I cannot) in a moment I do know   [blood,
Thou'dst call fair Temperance up to rule thy

    My husband, *and my* brother.] Sympson transposes the words thus :
        ' —— to see *Valetta,*
        ' My *brother,* and my *husband ;*'
again misunderstanding (we suppose, for he does it tacitly) *Valetta* to mean the *Grand-master,* not the city.

Thy eye was ever chaste, thy countenance
too, honest,
And all thy wooings was like maidens' talk.
Who yieldeth unto pleasures, and to lust,
Is a poor captive, that in golden fetters,
And precious, as he thinks, but holding gyves,
Frets out his life.
 Mir. Find such another woman,
And take her for his labour, any man!
 Ori. I was not worthy of thee, at my best,
(Heav'n knew I was not; I had had thee else)
Much less now, gentle sir. Miranda's deeds
Have been as white as Oriana's fame,
From the beginning to this point of time,
And shall we now begin to stain both thus?
Think on the legend which we two shall
breed,
Continuing as we are, for chastest dames
And boldest soldiers to peruse and read,
Ay, and read thorough, free from any act
To cause the modest cast the book away,
And the most honour'd captain fold it up.
 Mir. Fairest, let go my hand! my pulse
beats thick,   [vein!—
And my mov'd blood rides high in every
Lord of thyself now, soldier, and ever!
I would not for Aleppo, this frail bark,
This bark of flesh, no better steers-man had
Than has Mountferrat's.—May you kiss me,
lady?
 Ori. No; though't be no essential injury,
It is a circumstance due to my lord,
To none else; and, my dearest friend, if hands
Playing together kindle heat in you,
What may the game at lips provoke unto?
 Mir. Oh, what a tongue is here! Whilst
she doth teach
My heart to hate my fond unlawful love,
She talks me more in love, with love to her;
My fires she quencheth with her arguments,
But as she breathes 'em they blow fresher
 fires.—   [wife!
Sit further! now my flame cools. Husband!
There is some holy myst'ry in those names
That sure the unmarried cannot understand.
 Ori. Now thou art straight, and dost en-
  amour me
So far beyond a carnal earthly love,
My very soul dotes on thee, and my spirits
Do embrace thine; my mind doth thy mind
kiss;
And in this pure conjunction we enjoy
A heavenlier pleasure than if bodies met:
This, this is perfect love! the other short,
Yet languishing fruition. Ev'ry swain
And sweating groom may clasp, but ours re-
Two in ten ages cannot reach unto. [find
Nor is our spiritual love a barren joy;

For mark what blessed issue we'll beget,
(Dearer than children to posterity)
A great example to men's continence,
And women's chastity; that is a child
More fair and comfortable, than any heir!
 Mir. If all wives were but such, Lust would
not find
One corner to inhabit; sin would be
So strange, remission superfluous.—
But one petition, I have done.
 Ori. What, sweet?   [death
 Mir. To call me lord, if the hard hand of
Seize on Gomera first.
 Ori. Oh, much too worthy,
How much you undervalue your own price,
To give your unbought self for a poor woman,
That has been once sold, us'd, and lost her
show!
I am a garment worn, a vessel crack'd,
A zone untied, a lily trod upon,
A fragrant flower cropt by another's hand,
My colour sullied, and my odour chang'd.
If when I was new-blossom'd, I did fear
Myself unworthy of Miranda's spring,
Thus over-blown, and seeded, I am rather
Fit to adorn his chimney than his bed.
 Mir. Rise, miracle! save Malta with thy
virtue!   [spoke!
If words could make me proud, how has she
Yet I will try her to the very block.—
Hard-hearted and uncivil Oriana,
Ingrateful payer of my industries,
That with a soft painted hypocrisy
Cozen'st, and jeer'st my perturbation,
Expect a weighty and a fell revenge [35]
My comfort is, all men will think thee false:
Beside, thy husband, having been thus long
(On this occasion) in my fort, and power—

*Enter Norandine, Colonna, and Lucinda
with a Child.*

I'll hear no more words!—Captain, let's away!
With all care see to her; and you, Lucinda,
Attend her diligently: She's a wonder!
 Nor. Have you found she was well deli-
vered?
What, had she a good midwife? is all well?
 Mir. You're merry, Norandine.
 Luc. Why weep you, lady?
 Ori. Take the poor babe along.
 Col. Madam, 'tis here.
 Ori. Dissembling death, why didst thou
let me live
To see this change, my greatest cause to
grieve?   [Exeunt.

SCENE II.

[*Synnet, i. e. Flourish of trumpets* [36].

---

[35] *Expect a witty and a fell revenge.*] The coupling of these two epithets, perhaps, never
was from the Poet's pen. I am inclined to think that we have the same corruption here, as
in The Wild-Goose Chace; and that in both places we should read not *witty* but *weighty*.
                 Sympson.

[36] *Scene II. Enter Astorius, Castriot, Valetta, Gomera, Synnet, Knights, two Bishops,
Mountferrat guarded by Corporal and Soldiers, Abdella, a Gentleman with a cloak, sword, and
spurs; Gomera.*] This stage-direction corrected by Sympson.

*Enter Astorius, Castriot, Valetta, Gomera,
Knights, two Bishops, Mountferrat guarded
by Corporal and Soldiers, Abdella, a Gentleman with a cloak, sword, and spurs.*

Val. A tender husband hast thou shew'd
    thyself,
My dearest brother, and thy memory,
After thy life [37], in brazen characters
Shall monumentally be register'd
To ages consequent, till Time's running hand
Beats back the world to undistinguish'd
    chaos [38],
And on the top of that thy name shall stand
Fresh, and without decay.
  Gom. Oh, honour'd sir!
If hope of this, or any bliss to come,
Could lift my load of grief off from my soul,
Or expiate the trespass 'gainst my wife,
That in one hour's suspicion I begun,
I might be won to be a man again,
And fare like other husbands, sleep and eat,
Laugh, and forget my pleasing penitence;
But 'till old Nature can make such a wife
Again, I vow ne'er to resume the order
And habits that to men are necessary;
All breath I'll spend in sighs, all sound in
    groans,
And know no company but my wasting moans.
Asto. This will be wilful murder on yourself.
Nor like a Christian do you bear the chance
Which the inscrutable will of Heav'n admits.
  Gom. What would you have my weakness
    do, that
Suffer'd itself thus to be practis'd on
By a damn'd hell-hound, and his agent dam,
The impious midwife to abortive births,
And cruel instrument to his decrees?
By forgery they first assail'd her life,
Heav'n playing with us yet in that, he wrought
My dearest friend, the servant to her virtue,
To combat me, against his mistress' truth.
That yet effectless, this enchanting witch
Bred baneful jealousy against my lady, [her
My most immaculate lady, which seiz'd on
Almost to death. Oh, yet, not yet content,
She in my hand put (to restore her life,

As I imagin'd) what did execute   [child
Their dev'lish malice. Further, great with
Was this poor innocent: That too was lost;
They doubled death upon her! Not staying
    there,
They have done violence unto her tomb,
Not granting rest unto her in the grave.
I wish Miranda had enjoy'd my prize;
For sure I'm punish'd for usurping her.
Oh, what a tiger is resisted lust!
How it doth forage all!
  Mountf. Part of this tale   [her.
I grant you true; but 'twas not poison given
  Abd. I would it had! we had been far
    enough,
If we had been so wise; and had not now
Stood curt'sing for your mercies here.
  Mountf. Beside,
What is become o' th' body we know not.
  Val. Peace, impudents!
And, dear Gomera, practise patience,
As I myself must: By some means at last
We shall dissolve this riddle.
  Gom. Wherefore comes.
This villain in this festival array,
As if he triumph'd for his treachery?
  Cast. That is by our appointment: Give
    us leave;
You shall know why anon.

Enter Miranda, Norandine, and Colonna.

  Val. One of the Esguard [39].
  Esg. The gentlemen are come.
  Val. Truce then awhile.   [resolv'd?
With our sad thoughts!—What, are ye both
  Nor. Not I, my lord: Your down-right
    captain still
I'll live, and serve you. Not that altogether
I want compunction of conscience;
I have enough to save me, and that's all:
Bar me from drink, and drabs? ev'n hang
    me too!   [first!
You must ev'n make your captains capons
I have too much flesh for this spiritual knight-
    hood,
And therefore do desire forbearance, sir,

---

[37] *After my life.*] Amended by Sympson.

[38] ———— *till Time's running hand*
    Beats back the world to undistinguis'd chaos.] *Running* is, I allow, a proper epithet to
Time, but *Time's running hand beating the world to chaos*, does not seem to me a very clear
and consistent metaphor; and as *ruining* is so very near the trace of the letters, and appears
to have much more propriety and energy than the former, I think it bids fair for having been
the orignal.   *Seward.*

[39] *Val. One of th' Esguard.*

  Esg. The gentlemen are come.] Mr. Seward saw with me, that to put 'One of the *Esguard*'
into Valetta's mouth, was false and ridiculous. The stage direction was undoubtedly given
by our Authors thus:

Enter one of the Esguard.

  Esg. 'The gentlemen are come.
  Val. 'Truce then awhile
    'With your sad thoughts.'

Enter Miranda, Norandine and Colonna.

  'What, are you both resolv'd?' &c.'   *Sympson.*

'Till I am older, or more mortified;
I am too sound yet.
   Val. What say you, Miranda?
   Mir. With all pure zeal to Heaven, duty
to you,
I come to undergo it.
   Val. Proceed to th' ceremony.
   Gom. Before you match with this bright
honour'd title,
Admir'd Miranda, pardon that [40] in thought
I ever did transgress against your virtue;
And may you find more joy with your new
bride,
Than poor Gomera e'er enjoy'd with his!
(But 'twas mine own crime, and I suffer for't.)
Long wear your dignity, and worthily,
Whilst I obscurely in some corner vanish!
   Mir. Have stronger thoughts, and better.
—First, I crave,
According to the order of the court,
I may dispose my captives, and the fort,
That with a clean and purified heart
The fitlier I may indue my robe.
   All. 'Tis granted.

*Enter Oriana veil'd, Ladies, Lucinda with a
Child.*

   Mir. Bring the captives!—To your charge
And staid tuition, my most noble friend,
I then commend this lady. Start not off!
A fairer and a chaster never liv'd.
By her own choice you are her guardian;
For telling her I was to leave my fort,
And to abandon quite all worldly cares,
Her own request was, to Gomera's hands
She might be giv'n in custody, for sh' had
heard
He was a gentleman, wise, and temperate,
Full of humanity to women-kind,
And, 'cause he had been married, knew the
better
How to entreat a lady.
   Val. What countrywoman is she?
   Mir. Born a Greek,
   Val. Gomera, 'twill be barbarous to deny
A lady, that unto your refuge flies,
And seeks to shroud her under Virtue's wing.
   Gom. Excuse me, noble sir! Oh, think me
So dull a devil [40], to forget the loss   [not
Of such a matchless wife as I possess'd,
And ever to endure the sight of woman!
Were she the abstract of her sex for form,
The only warehouse of perfection,
Were there no rose nor lily but her cheek,
No musick but her tongue, virtue but hers,
She must not rest near me. My vow is graven
Here in my heart, irrevocably breath'd;
And when I break it——
   Asto. This is rudeness, Spaniard;

Unseasonably you play the Timonist [41],
Put on a disposition is not yours,
Which neither fits you, nor becomes you.
   Gom. Sir——   [persuade.
   Cast. We cannot force you, but we would
   Gom. Beseech you, sir, no more! I am
resolv'd
To forsake Malta, tread a pilgrimage
To fair Jerusalem, for my lady's soul,
And will not be diverted.
   Mir. You must bear
This child along wi'ye then.
   Gom. What child?
   All. How's this?   [ous!
   Mir. Nay then, Gomera, thou'rt injuri-
This child is thine, and this rejected lady
Thou hast as often known as thine own wife;
And this I'll make good on thee, with my
sword.
   Gom. Thou durst as well blaspheme!—If
such a scandal—
(I crave the rights due to a gentleman)
Woman, unveil!
   Ori. Will you refuse me yet? [*Unveiling.*
   Gom. My wife!
   Val. My sister!
   Gom. Somebody thank Heav'n!
I cannot speak.
   All. All praise be ever giv'n!
   Mountf. This saves our lives. Yet 'would
she had been dead!
The very sight of her afflicts me more
Than fear of punishment, or my disgrace.
   Val. How came you to the temple?
   Mir. Sir, to do
My poor devotions, and to offer thanks
For scaping a temptation near perform'd
With this fair virgin.—I restore a wife
Earth cannot parallel; and, busy Nature,
If thou wilt still make women, but remember
To work 'em by this sampler!—Take heed,
Henceforth you never doubt, sir,   [sir,
   Gom. When I do,
Death take me suddenly!
   Mir. To encrease your happiness,
To your best wife take this addition.
   Gom. Alack, my poor knave!
      [*To the Child.*
   Val. The confession
The Moor made, it seems, was truth.   [ever
   Nor. Marry was it, sir; the only truth that
Issued out of hell, which her black jaws re-
semble.   [giving
A plague o' your bacon-face! you must be
Drinks, with a vengeance! Ah, thou branded
bitch!
Do you stare, goggles? I hope to make
Winter-boots o' thy hide yet; she fears not
dunning!

---

   [40] *Pardon what in thought.*] So the former editions.
   [40] *So dull a devil.*] Seward proposes reading, *so* FULL *a devil*; '*i. e.*' (says he) ' Think me
' not so *altogether* a devil as to forget the worth of her I have killed. The use of *full* in this
' manner I could give many instances of.' This, however, we much doubt.
   [41] *Timonist.*] *i. e.* Timon of Athens, alluding to the misanthropy of that character.

Hell-fire can't parch her blacker than she is.
Do you grin, chimney-sweeper?

Ori. What is't, Miranda?

Mir. That you would please Lucinda might
attend you.

Col. That suit, sir, I consent not to.

Luc. My husband?
My dearest Angelo?

Nor. More jiggam-bobs? Is not this the
fellow that　　　　　　　　　　　[vice?
Swam like a duck to the shore in our sea-ser-

Col. The very same. Do not you know me
now, sir?
My name is Angelo, tho' Colonna veil'd it,
Your countryman and kinsman, born in Flo-
rence;
Who from the neighbour-island here of Goza
Was captive led, in that unfortunate day
When the Turk bore with him three thousand
souls.
Since, in Constantinople have I liv'd,
Where I beheld this Turkish damsel first.
A tedious suitor was I for her love;　　[hide
And, pitying such a beauteous case should
A soul prophan'd with infidelity,
I labour'd her conversion, with my love,
And doubly won her : To fair faith her soul
She first betroth'd, and then her faith to me.
But fearful there to consummate this contract,
We fled, and in that flight were ta'en again
By those same gallies 'fore Valetta fought:
Since, in your service I attended here,
Where, what I saw and heard hath joy'd me
more
Than all my past afflictions griev'd before.

Val. Wonders crown wonders! Take thy
wife.—Miranda,
Be henceforth call'd our Malta's better angel;
And thou her evil, Mountferrat.　　[black

Nor. We'll call him Cacodemon, with his
Gib there, his Succuba, his devil's seed,
His spawn of Phlegethon, that, o' my con-
science,
Was bred o' th' spume of Cocytus.—Do you
snarl, you black Gill?
She looks like the picture of America.

Val. Why stay we now?

Mir. This last petition to the court;
I may bequeath the keeping of my fort
To this my kinsman, tow'rd the maintenance
Of him and his fair virtuous wife : Discreet,
Loyal, and valiant, I dare give him you.

Val. You must not ask in vain, sir.

Col. My best thanks
To you, my noble cousin, and my service
To the whole court: May I deserve this bounty!

Val. Proceed to th' ceremony. One of our
Degrade Mountferrat first!　　　[Esguard

Mountf. I will not sue
For mercy; 'twere in vain: Fortune, thy
worst!　　　　　　　　　　　[Musick.

*An altar discover'd, with tapers and a book on
it. The two Bishops stand on each side of
it; Mountferrat, as the song is singing,
ascends up the altar.*

See, see, the stain of honour, Virtue's foe,
Of virgins' fair fames the foul overthrow!
That broken hath his oath of chastity,
Dishonour'd much this holy dignity;
Off with his robe, expel him forth this
place,　　　　　　　　　　　[grace!
Whilst we rejoice, and sing at his dis-

Val. Since by thy actions thou hast made
thyself
Unworthy of that worthy sign thou wear'st,
And of our sacred order, into which
For former virtues we receiv'd thee first,
According to our statutes, ordinances,
For praise unto the good, a terror to
The bad, and an example to all men;
We here deprive thee of our habit, and
Declare thee unworthy our society,
From which we do expel thee, as a rotten,
Corrupted, and contagious member.

Esg. Using th' authority the superior
Hath giv'n unto me, I untie this knot,
And take from thee the pleasing yoke of
Heaven:
We take from off thy breast this holy cross,
Which thou hast made thy burden, not thy
prop;
Thy spurs we spoil thee of, leaving thy heels
Bare of thy honour[41], that have kick'd against
Our order's precepts; next we reave thy
sword,
And give thee armless to thy enemies,
For being foe to goodness, and to God;
Last, 'bout thy stiff neck we this halter hang,
And leave thee to the mercy of the court.

Val. Invest Miranda[42].

SONG.

Fair child of Virtue, Honour's bloom,
That here with burning zeal dost come,
With joy to ask the white-cross cloak,
And yield unto this pleasing yoke!
That being young, vows chastity,
And chusest wilful poverty;
As this flame mounts, so mount thy zeal!
thy glory　　　　　　　　　　[story!
Rise past the stars, and fix in Heav'n thy

1 Bishop. What crave you, gentle sir?

Mir. Humble admittance
To be a brother of the holy hospital
Of great Jerusalem.

2 Bishop. Breathe out your vow.

Mir. To Heav'n, and all the bench of
saints above,
(Whose succour I implore t' enable me)
I vow henceforth a chaste life; not to enjoy
Any thing proper to myself; obedience

---

[41] *Bare of thy honour.*] Sympson thinks we should read, ' bare of *their* honour.'

[42] *Invest Miranda.*] The ceremonies of receiving a knight into the order of Malta, may be seen at large in Vertot's History of the Knights of Malta, vol. vi. p. 18. R.

To my superiors, whom religion
And Heav'n shall give me; ever to defend
The virtuous fame of Jadies, and to oppugn
E'en unto death the Christian enemy:
This do I vow t'accomplish!

  Ang. Who can tell,
Has he made other vow, or promis'd marriage
To any one, or is in servitude?

  All. He's free from all these.

  1 Bishop. Put on his spurs, and gird him
    with the sword,
The scourge of infidels, and types of speed.
Buildest thy faith on this?
               [*Presenting the cross.*

  Mir. On him that died
On such a sacred figure, for our sins.

  2 Bishop. Here then we fix it on thy left
    side, for   [service
Thy increase of faith, Christian defence, and
To th' poor; and thus near to thy heart we
    plant it,   [heart;
That thou mayst love it ev'n with all thy
With thy right hand protect, preserve it
  whole;
For if thou fighting 'gainst Heav'n's enemies
Shalt fly away, abandoning the cross,
The ensign of thy holy general,
With shame thou justly shalt be robb'd of it,

Chas'd from our company, and cut away
As an infectious putrified limb.

  Mir. I ask no favour.

  1 Bishop. Then receive the yoke
Of him that makes it sweet and light; in which,
Thy soul find her eternal rest!

  Val. Most welcome!

  All. Welcome, our noble brother!

  Val. Break up the court.—Mountferrat,
    tho' your deeds,
Conspiring 'gainst the lives of innocents,
Have forfeited your own, we will not stain
Our white cross with your blood: Your doom
  is then
To marry this co-agent of your mischiefs;
Which done, we banish you to th' continent [44]:
If either, after three days, here be found,
The hand of law lays hold upon your lives.

  Nor. Away, French stallion! Now
You have a Barbary mare of your own; go
  leap her,
And engender young devilings!

  Val. We will find something, noble No-
  randine,
To quit your merit.—So, to civil feasts,
According to our customs; and all pray
The dew of grace bless our new Knight to-
  day!   [*Exeunt omnes.*

---

[44] *We banish you the continent.*] Would not one think, though they are here in an island,
that they were actually upon the continent? Certainly the English of our days, and that of
our Poets, has undergone great alterations, if we ought not to read by a small addition,

    '———— we banish you *to th'* continent.'   *Sympson.*

Also from Benediction Books ...

Wandering Between Two Worlds: Essays on Faith and Art
Anita Mathias
Benediction Books, 2007
152 pages
ISBN: 0955373700

Available from www.amazon.com, www.amazon.co.uk
www.wanderingbetweentwoworlds.com

In these wide-ranging lyrical essays, Anita Mathias writes, in lush, lovely prose, of her naughty Catholic childhood in Jamshedpur, India; her large, eccentric family in Mangalore, a sea-coast town converted by the Portuguese in the sixteenth century; her rebellion and atheism as a teenager in her Himalayan boarding school, run by German missionary nuns, St. Mary's Convent, Nainital; and her abrupt religious conversion after which she entered Mother Teresa's convent in Calcutta as a novice. Later rich, elegant essays explore the dualities of her life as a writer, mother, and Christian in the United States-- Domesticity and Art, Writing and Prayer, and the experience of being "an alien and stranger" as an immigrant in America, sensing the need for roots.

About the Author

Anita Mathias was born in India, has a B.A. and M.A. in English from Somerville College, Oxford University and an M.A. in Creative Writing from the Ohio State University. Her essays have been published in The Washington Post, The London Magazine, The Virginia Quarterly Review, Commonweal, Notre Dame Magazine, America, The Christian Century, Religion Online, The Southwest Review, Contemporary Literary Criticism, New Letters, The Journal, and two of HarperSanFrancisco's The Best Spiritual Writing anthologies. Her non-fiction has won fellowships from The National Endowment for the Arts; The Minnesota State Arts Board; The Jerome Foundation, The Vermont Studio Center; The Virginia Centre for the Creative Arts, and the First Prize for the Best General Interest Article from the Catholic Press Association of the United States and Canada. Anita has taught Creative Writing at the College of William and Mary, and now lives and writes in Oxford, England.

"Yesterday's Treasures for Today's Readers"

Titles by Benediction Classics available from Amazon.co.uk

Religio Medici, Hydriotaphia, Letter to a Friend, Thomas Browne

Pseudodoxia Epidemica: Or, Enquiries into Commonly Presumed Truths, Thomas Browne

The Maid's Tragedy, Beaumont and Fletcher

The Custom of the Country, Beaumont and Fletcher

Philaster Or Love Lies a Bleeding, Beaumont and Fletcher

A Treatise of Fishing with an Angle,   Dame Juliana Berners.

Pamphilia to Amphilanthus, Lady Mary Wroth

The Compleat Angler, Izaak Walton

The Magnetic Lady, Ben Jonson

Every Man Out of His Humour, Ben Jonson

The Masque of Blacknesse. The Masque of Beauty,. Ben Jonson

The Life of St. Thomas More, William Roper

Pendennis, William Makepeace Thackeray

Salmacis and Hermaphroditus attributed to Francis Beaumont

Friar Bacon and Friar Bungay Robert Greene

Holy Wisdom, Augustine Baker

The Jew of Malta and the Massacre at Paris, Christopher Marlowe

Tamburlaine the Great, Parts 1 & 2 AND Massacre at Paris, Christopher Marlowe

All Ovids Elegies, Lucans First Booke, Dido Queene of Carthage, Hero and Leander, Christopher Marlowe

The Titan, Theodore Dreiser

Trilogy of Desire: "The Financier" , "The Titan" and "The Stoic", Theodore Dreiser

Scapegoats of the Empire: The true story of the Bushveldt Carbineers, George Witton

All Hallows' Eve, Charles Williams

Descent into Hell, Charles Williams

My Apprenticeship: Volumes I and II, Beatrice Webb

Last and First Men / Star Maker, Olaf Stapledon

Darkness and the Light, Olaf Stapledon

The Worst Journey in the World, Apsley Cherry-Garrard

The Schoole of Abuse, Containing a Pleasaunt Invective Against Poets, Pipers, Plaiers, Iesters and Such Like Catepillers of the Commonwelth, Stephen Gosson

Russia in the Shadows, H. G. Wells

Wild Swans at Coole, W. B. Yeats

A hundreth good pointes of husbandrie, Thomas Tusser

The Collected Works of Nathanael West: "The Day of the Locust", "The Dream Life of Balso Snell", "Miss Lonelyhearts", "A Cool Million", Nathanael West

Miss Lonelyhearts & The Day of the Locust, Nathaniel West

The Worst Journey in the World, Apsley Cherry-Garrard

Scott's Last Expedition, V1, R. F. Scott

The Herries Chronicle: Rogue Herries, Judith Paris, The Fortress and Vanessa, Hugh Walpole

Rogue Herries, Hugh Walpole

Judith Paris, Hugh Walpole

The Fortress, Hugh Walpole

Vanessa, Hugh Walpole

The Dream of Gerontius, John Henry Newman

The Brother of Daphne, Dornford Yates

The Poetry of Architecture: Or the Architecture of the Nations of Europe Considered in Its Association with Natural Scenery and National Character, John Ruskin

The Downfall of Robert Earl of Huntington, Anthony Munday

Clayhanger, Arnold Bennett

South: The Story of Shackleton's Last Expedition 1914-1917, Sir Ernest Shackketon

The Bishop and Other Stories, Anton Chekov

Greene's Groatsworth of Wit: Bought With a Million of Repentance, Robert Greene

Beau Sabreur, Percival Christopher Wren

The Hekatompathia, or Passionate Centurie of Love, Thomas Watson

The Road to Wigan Pier, George Orwell

The Art of Rhetoric, Thomas Wilson

Stepping Heavenward, Elizabeth Prentiss

Barker's Delight, or The Art of Angling, Thomas Barker

9 781849 021708